Praise for Wellbeing in the Primary Classroom

'This is a wonderfully humane and useful book for teachers. Idea by idea it shows how the skills for living can be taught in practice. Beautifully written by a teacher who walks the talk.'

Lord Richard Layard, Chairman of Action for Happiness, @actionhappiness

'Children's mental wellbeing is so vitally important. Happier children learn more, cope better and are much more likely to make the most of their potential. Adrian Bethune is an inspiration and this book should be required reading for everyone involved in teaching young children. It's a perfect blend of scientific research, real-world experience and practical ideas that really make a difference. Highly recommended.'

Dr Mark Williamson, Director of Action for Happiness, @actionhappiness

'I can't wait for this book to be published! Adrian Bethune really knows how to condense the hard stuff and make it clear. The mindfulness chapter, in particular, is great and answers so many questions people might have.'

Ruby Wax, Writer, Performer and Poster Girl for Mental Health, @Rubywax

'Empirically researched and scientific, yet practical and accessible. What makes this book so refreshing is Adrian's authenticity. He practises this stuff day in day out and the impact is evident in the children he teaches. If this was on the reading list for all newly qualified teachers, imagine the difference it could make!'

Yvonne Biggins, MAPP, Co-Founder of Young Happy Minds, @YoungHappyMinds

Wellbeing in the Primary Classroom

Other titles from Bloomsbury Education

100 Ideas for Primary Teachers: Mindfulness in the Classroom,
by Tammie Prince

Mental Health Matters, by Paula Nagel

Teaching Happiness and Well-Being in Schools, by Ian Morris

Live Well, Teach Well: A practical approach to wellbeing that works,
by Abigail Mann

How to Survive in Teaching: Without imploding, exploding or walking away,
by Dr Emma Kell

Teach, Reflect, Doodle, by Paul Wright

Wellbeing in the Primary Classroom

A practical guide to teaching happiness

Adrian Bethune

BLOOMSBURY EDUCATION

LONDON OXFORD NEW YORK NEW DELHI SYDNEY

Bloomsbury Education
Bloomsbury Publishing Plc
50 Bedford Square, London, WC1B 3DP, UK

BLOOMSBURY, BLOOMSBURY EDUCATION and the Diana logo are
trademarks of Bloomsbury Publishing Plc

First published in Great Britain 2018

A catalogue record for this book is available from the British Library.

ISBN: PB: 978-1-4729-5154-0; ePDF: 978-1-4729-5156-4;
ePub: 978-1-4729-5155-7

2 4 6 8 10 9 7 5 3 (paperback)

Typeset by Newgen KnowledgeWorks Pvt. Ltd., Chennai, India
Printed and bound by CPI Group (UK) Ltd., Croydon CR0 4YY

To find out more about our authors and books visit www.bloomsbury.com
and sign up for our newsletters.

This book is dedicated to Samantha, Eli and Raif.

You make me happy.

Contents

Acknowledgements

Writing this book has genuinely been a huge privilege and an absolute joy (OK, and sometimes a real slog!). I still cannot quite believe I am a published author. But this dream would certainly not have become a reality if it weren't for some very special people who I'd like to give thanks to.

First of all, my friends and family. To my wife Sam, before I'd even contacted publishers about my idea for a book, I gave you my 'Preface' to read. I was nervous about you reading it and was expecting lots of corrections and suggestions. You simply said, 'I love it! It's great!' That honestly gave me the confidence and courage I needed to keep writing and take my ideas further. You have kindly and patiently read every single word I've written and your feedback has been invaluable. I could not have written this book without your support.

Thank you to my parents who looked after my son, Eli, every Wednesday so I could write. Knowing he was happy with his 'Ooma' and 'Oompa' allowed me to immerse myself in my work. And to my son Eli, thank you for increasing the length of your naps at a time when I really needed to knuckle down with the book! Thank you to my parents-in-law, Mike and Celia – when I first started teaching, you bought me books on child psychology and attachment theory. Those books have not only influenced my teaching but are also the backbone of this book! Finally, to my best friend, Joe. Over drinks I told you about my idea for my book and that I was going to contact Bloomsbury to see if they'd be interested in it. 'I know someone who works there,' you replied, and before I could procrastinate and probably never follow through with my plan, you'd emailed your friend who asked to see my proposal. I had no chance to back out then, so thanks!

To all the lovely staff at Bloomsbury. Thank you first to former commissioning editor, Miriam Davey. You were leaving Bloomsbury when I first contacted you and so should have been on wind-down mode and not doing any real work, but you believed in my book proposal and got it approved just days before you left. I am so very grateful you did that! Thanks to Laura Neate for the cover design, which I love! And last but not least, to my editor, Hannah Marston, thank you for your honest feedback, ideas and suggestions. You too have believed in me and this book, and your enthusiasm has spurred me on and kept me going!

Every chapter of this book has been read by an expert from the fields of wellbeing, psychology and neuroscience. I wanted to ensure the facts, statistics, claims, evidence, and research was as accurate as it could be. I am indebted to your feedback, expertise and wise counsel. Thank you to Rick Hanson, Louis Cozolino, Ruby Wax, Debbie Johnson, Mark Williamson, Vanessa King, Peter Harper, John Ratey, Emma Kell, Yvonne Biggins, Vicki Zakrzewski and Tal Ben-Shahar for reading my chapters. Thank you also to Sir Anthony Seldon for writing such a fabulous foreword for this book.

Finally, I would like to thank Sue Harte and Suzanne Stace, two maverick heads who put wellbeing ahead of data, as well as all of the children, parents and staff from John Stainer and Westfield Primary schools. You are the main inspiration and this book is for you!

Adrian

Foreword

I am very pleased to be writing this foreword for such an important and timely publication. Although my experience of teaching has been mostly at secondary and now at university level, the case for making wellbeing a major priority at primary school is evident to me.

The roots of the current serious and troubling epidemic of mental health issues can be found in the earliest years, and over the several years spent in primary school, children's mental health and wellbeing are not always prioritised as they should be. Teachers are under pressure to show progress across the curriculum and achieve results in SATs and GCSEs, sometimes at the expense of their own wellbeing and the children in their care.

In this helpful and practical book, Adrian Bethune examines a positive approach to mental health and wellbeing at primary level. He begins by examining the theory and scientific justification for such an approach and then gives practical advice and strategies for teachers to try out in the classroom.

Based on his own experience of teaching different year groups at primary level and with a series of case studies based on this experience, the practices of creating a tribal classroom, gratitude, mindfulness, physical exercise and the wellbeing of staff as well as pupils are examined in detail and then helpfully summarised for the harassed and busy teacher to return to and put into practice.

I do not know a single teacher or leader in primary schools who does not care for the wellbeing of the children in their charge. The issue is not whether they care or not, but one of finding the time and having the information about how to make wellbeing interventions effective. Let us be clear; prioritising wellbeing of children at school, if done properly, enhances their academic performance rather than detracts from it. It creates a better atmosphere in school and improves behaviour. It means better teacher wellbeing. What is there not to like about all of this? Reading this book is not only practical and important, it will also make schools better by far.

Sir Anthony Seldon
Vice-Chancellor of the University of Buckingham
Former Master of Wellington College

Preface

Our best chance for happiness is education.

— Mark Van Doren

In my late twenties, life was going pretty well for me. I had a good job in music publishing and a decent social life. Around this time, I bought my first flat, and things were progressing nicely with my girlfriend. Life was good. But then things started to unravel, unexpectedly. A big fall out with a close friend knocked me, and breaking up with my girl-friend left me feeling lonely and isolated in my new flat. A period of acute anxiety followed, which turned into a bout of depression. I had never experienced anything like this before and I didn't know what to do. As someone who had worked very hard at school and university, I remember thinking to myself at one point, 'I have all of this knowledge and learning, but none of it is helping me get better.' I just didn't have the answers to my problems, and I wasn't sure where to turn.

Fortunately, supportive family and friends helped me through the worst of it, and I was able to seek help in the form of a counsellor. I started to read about the causes of anxiety and depression, and learned how to take better care of my physical and mental health. I began exer-cising more, eating more healthily, and I dipped my toes in the water of meditation. This experience taught me the absolute importance of looking after your mental health. It also made me reflect more generally about what I was doing with my life.

Although my work was fun, fairly interesting and I was paid well, something was missing. I guess it was meaning. My job didn't feel like it was really making the world a better place. So, whilst still working in the music industry, I signed up to a mentoring scheme with a charity called Chance UK. I was matched with a nine-year-old boy in Hackney (let's call him Wesley) who was being taught in a behaviour unit because he would often become violent and aggressive at his school. After work and on the weekends, I would meet up with Wesley and take him to the local park, to the library, to museums, the cinema, anywhere really. The idea was that I'd be a positive male role model in his life and we'd set little goals to achieve each week to give his life some direction and purpose. It was extremely challenging at times. Like the time when a gang fight was just about to break out in the park where we were playing football. Or, when I had to rush round to Wesley's house to console him after a boy in his behaviour unit took his own life. But it was also immensely rewarding. My life had a lot more meaning when I was mentoring Wesley. I got to know a lovely young boy whose home life (absent father, mother with depression, older teenage brother involved in local gangs) was a big reason why he was angry, and his school was not really helping him. After a year of mentoring Wesley, our time together came to an end and he graduated from the mentoring scheme. By the time we parted company, he was signed up to a local football team, he was taking part in weekly martial arts classes and was back in a new mainstream school and seemingly doing well.

About the same time, a good friend of mine called Ros asked me if I would volunteer to be a school governor at the local primary school she taught at. I agreed and enjoyed seeing how a school was run and felt like I was genuinely contributing to my local community. Both the mentoring and school governing made me reflect on my career. I wanted a job where I gave something back every day. I wanted a job where I could make a difference every day. I wanted to help the other Wesleys in our school system fit in, be happy and be a success. In 2010, I decided to retrain to become a primary school teacher. Michael Gove had just become the Education Secretary. Nightmare!

It really didn't take me long to realise that my dream of making a difference to young people was not going to happen in the way I had envisaged. With a relentless focus on children's academic progress, the education system had changed a lot since I had been at school. The curriculum was so packed there didn't seem to be time to deal with children's friendship issues or emotional concerns. It was all about pace, progress and next steps. No time to be happy. Schools aren't judged on the wellbeing of their pupils. Ofsted doesn't scrutinise happiness data. Within my first year of teaching I thought I'd made a big mistake and considered quitting several times.

Fortunately, two fortuitous things happened at about the same time. Firstly, a teacher training friend of mine, Lowri, lent me the book *Teaching Happiness and Well-Being in Schools* by Ian Morris. As I read the book during my Easter holidays, I remember thinking to myself, 'YES! This is what teaching should be about! This is why I became a teacher! You *can* teach children how to be happier and to help them flourish.' Although the book was set in a secondary context, I started to think of ways of using some of the ideas in my classroom. And then, one morning whilst reading the book, I chanced upon an item on the BBC News about the launch of an organisation called 'Action for Happiness' – a charity helping people to take action to make the world a happier place. The launch was happening that day in London. I jumped on my bike and cycled as fast as I could to get to the launch event.

I didn't have a ticket to the sold-out event and had to blag my way in. I just caught the end of Sir Anthony Seldon's talk about how our education system is broken, that most schools are exam factories and that we should be teaching children how to lead happier lives. It was music to my ears! I signed up to become a member of Action for Happiness and made my pledge – 'To make a more conscious effort to choose a more positive, compassionate and happy frame of mind which, in turn, I hope becomes infectious!' From that day on, I vowed to make my classroom the happiest place it could be for me and my children, and to then try to influence the rest of the school. Eventually, I had designs to revolutionise the whole UK education system, but I was in my first year of teaching and I needed to pace myself.

Those two events have set me on my teaching happiness journey. Along the way, I've read lots of books about the brain and the science of happiness. I've completed various courses in mindfulness and positive psychology. I've experimented in my classroom with various ideas and had some great successes and some abject failures. I've experienced many serendipitous encounters since focusing my teaching practice on the happiness and wellbeing of my pupils. I got Eamonn Holmes and his panel to meditate live on Sky Breakfast News, and spoke in front of 2,500 people on stage with His Holiness, the Dalai Lama (see Figure 0.1, p. xviii). All of this through teaching happiness in primary schools! But, most importantly, I feel I've been able to positively impact the lives of the children in my care by teaching them life-affirming skills.

Figure 0.1: Three former pupils and me on stage with His Holiness, the Dalai Lama. Reproduced with kind permission from Action for Happiness

This book aims to be a practical guide for how you can teach primary school-aged children to be happier. The ideas are backed up by science and research and I have tried them in my classroom (and so have many other teachers too). This is not a one-size-fits-all book. You may need to tweak and adapt the ideas to suit your school, your class and your children. Some of the ideas may work wonderfully, others may not. The whole point is to take action and experiment. If you don't, nothing changes and we are still left with the broken system we had before.

There is a quote I love by Ralph Waldo Emerson that has informed a lot of my teaching practice: 'Do not be too timid and squeamish about your actions. All life is an experiment. The more experiments you make, the better.' This book is a guide and an invitation to be bold and experiment with some new ideas in your classrooms. I wish you luck and success on your teaching happiness journey.

Adrian Bethune, 2018

Introduction

Educators – parents and teachers – who care about helping children lead happy lives must first themselves believe that happiness is the ultimate currency.

— Tal Ben-Shahar, 2008

There are many people who would argue that our education system is outdated and not fit for purpose. And I have to say that I would agree with them. Created during the Industrial Revolution of the 19th century, our school system was designed to give people skills that were essential for them to succeed in an industrial world. Children were taught how to master the technical skills of reading, writing and calculation. Although these skills are still important now, the world our children are growing up in has changed, whereas our school system has not. And change is continuing and rapid. We have been focusing so hard on filling our children's heads that we may have forgotten about their hearts. I am in favour of a 'knowledge-rich curriculum' but is the knowledge we are currently teaching our children in schools what they need to lead well-rounded and happy lives?

High-stakes testing and an extremely narrow curriculum (with just English and maths assessed at a national level in primary schools), where all children are expected to make linear progress year after year, not only put teachers and children under huge pressures but sap the life out of teaching and education. As one adage puts it, 'Schools should prepare children for the tests of life, not a life of tests.' I believe schools could be so much more than this. They could be places of self-discovery, places of wonder and awe. Schools should nurture our youngest people and respect and value their unique differences. Schools should help children uncover their immense potential and enable them to realise that they can have a positive impact on the world. I believe that teaching happiness and wellbeing in primary schools is one way to achieve this. Teaching happiness has benefits for teachers too. Teaching the skills of wellbeing brings humanity back to education, it can rekindle teachers' passion for educating young people and it can restore the innate meaning and purpose to teaching that comes from wanting to make a difference in children's lives.

What is happiness and wellbeing?

What happiness is and how to 'obtain' it has been debated for millennia. There are of course individual differences in what happiness means to people. For example, I get a great deal of pleasure and purpose from working with young people as a teacher. But, for others, the thought of working with children every day is a complete nightmare. However, research shows that there are some common themes that appear to contribute to most people's happiness, such as having strong social ties and contributing to something bigger than yourself. Psychologists can sometimes get quite technical when it comes to happiness and rather than calling it as such, prefer to use terms like 'subjective wellbeing' and 'psychological wellbeing'. Subjective wellbeing is a person's own assessment of how well their life, or specific aspects of it, are going. Two commonly used measures of 'subjective wellbeing' are life satisfaction and the experience of positive and negative emotions. Psychological wellbeing is concerned with people's sense of meaning, purpose and engagement with life. Working towards these may not bring pleasure (positive emotions) at the time, but leads to a sense of fulfilment longer term. When we have high subjective and psychological wellbeing, by some definitions we may be said to be flourishing (The Children's Society, 2016).

For the purposes of this book, we'll keep the definition of happiness and wellbeing nice and simple, and I use the terms interchangeably to mean the same thing:

Living a life where one regularly experiences positive emotions (like joy, peace, love, curiosity, fun), feels that, overall, life is going well, together with feeling engaged in work and interests, and having a sense of meaning and purpose.

I think it is important to point out that the happiness I am focusing on in this book is not about feeling good all the time. This is unrealistic. We can actually make ourselves feel less happy if we're always trying to feel great because this is an unachievable goal. We will all experience loss, heartache, anxiety and loneliness at times. These feelings are normal reactions to life's difficulties and they can help us grow. We become wiser by learning to navigate through the rocky terrains of life. Without difficulties, we cannot hope to develop our levels of resilience, which is a core part of leading a happy life.

So, happiness involves all the emotions, not just positive ones. In fact, a recent study showed that even negative emotions like anger can make us feel 'happy' if these were the emotions we desired to feel at that time (Tamir et al., 2017). The lead researcher in this study, Dr Maya Tamir said, 'Happiness is more than simply feeling pleasure and avoiding pain. Happiness is about having experiences that are meaningful and valuable, including emotions that you think are the right ones to have.' (American Psychological Association, 2017)

Importantly, our happiness is something we have to work at regularly. It is not a destination you arrive at and that's it. You wouldn't go to the gym for a month and then sit back and relax for the rest of your life enjoying your new-found levels of fitness. And so it is with our happiness – it takes work and effort, and it is a journey that will last us our whole rich, diverse and messy lives.

Can you teach happiness?

There used to be a commonly held belief that people's happiness levels were determined from birth and didn't really change much during our adult lives. The 'set point theory' argued that people were either born with a sunny disposition or not, and that despite good or bad events happening to you, your happiness levels would always return to their 'set point' (Lykken and Tellegen, 1996). These researchers gave examples of people whose happiness levels returned to their 'set point' after dramatic life events, such as winning the lottery or becoming a paraplegic (Brickman et al., 1978).

Although it is certainly true that genes (and our early upbringing) do play a part, the latest research shows that there is a lot we can do to impact and change our levels of happiness and wellbeing in the long term (in effect, raising our 'set point' of happiness). Research by psychology professor, Sonja Lyubomirsky (Lyubomirsky et al., 2005), studied identical twins, separated at birth and raised in different places and by different parents, to see the role genetics play in our happiness levels. If genes determined our happiness levels from birth, then the identical twins studied (who have a 100 per cent DNA match) should have been as happy as one another, but this was not the case. Lyubomirsky's research concluded that genetics only determined their happiness levels by up to 50 per cent.

Furthermore, she discovered that people's life circumstances (gender, race, where they lived, etc.), assuming their basic needs, such as food and safety, were met, had less impact on happiness than we might think – in this study accounting, on average, for around ten per cent, with this relatively small amount being due to 'adaptation' to these factors. Adaptation is when people get used to a new situation or thing (e.g. the place they live, or the new car they bought), and the joy or misery it first provoked wanes and we adapt to it and our happiness levels return back to our 'set point'.

However, the most interesting discovery of Lyubomirsky's research was that a whopping 40 per cent of happiness was determined by the choices and actions the participants took.

By monitoring very happy people, Lyubomirsky and other psychologists have been able to identify the intentional activities and strategies that work to boost and maintain people's levels of happiness (Sheldon and Lyubomirsky, 2007). There were common themes that arose when happy people's lives, behaviours and thinking were scrutinised. According to Lyubomirsky, in general, happy people tend to:

- invest a lot into their close personal relationships with friends and family
- express high levels of gratitude for what they have
- be quite helpful and altruistic
- have an optimistic outlook when imagining their future
- savour pleasures and tend to live in the present moment
- exercise regularly
- have a clear sense of purpose in life (Lyubomirsky, 2006).

Lyubomirsky and other psychologists' research certainly suggests that you can teach happiness and you can learn to be happier. This relatively new area of psychology is known as positive psychology (Seligman and Csikszentmihalyi, 2000). Whereas traditional psychology focuses on illness, misery and people's 'issues', positive psychologists study how human beings flourish and what contributes to a happy and meaningful life.

Perhaps happiness is best thought of as a skill. It is something we need to practise, to hone and to craft. As the Dalai Lama says, 'Happiness is not something ready-made. It comes from your own actions.' So, alongside the skills of reading, writing and maths, we can add skills for happiness. This book delves into these skills in more detail and shows you how to teach them to children.

Why teach happiness in schools?

It's all very well and good that positive psychology is proving that we can teach ourselves to be happier, but why on earth should it be taught in schools? Surely schools are where academic rigour and study take place, not where we learn how to be more grateful or be more mindful? What's the point in wasting the children's time reflecting on what went well for them when they need to be learning how to use relative clauses, modal verbs and the subjunctive (for the record, I am still not entirely sure what these are!). There can sometimes be much eye-rolling and guffawing when you talk about teaching happiness in schools. But there are several important arguments for why it should be done.

Wellbeing and attainment

If a school wants to improve the academic performance of its pupils, it should, first and foremost, focus on their happiness and wellbeing. The simple fact is that pupils with higher levels of wellbeing generally perform better at school academically (Gutman and Vorhaus, 2012). Evidence shows that schools that put in place programmes to boost pupils' social and emotional skills have an 11 per cent gain in attainment, as well as improvements in pupil behaviour (Durlak et al., 2011). Conversely, low wellbeing is linked with poor academic performance at school, and children with emotional and behavioural difficulties are more likely to be excluded from school, or leave without any qualifications (Parry-Langdon, 2008). Public Health England published a report in 2014 entitled *The Link Between Pupil Health and Wellbeing and Attainment* and it strongly made the case for more headteachers, governors and teachers placing a greater focus on the wellbeing of their pupils, especially if they wanted to raise attainment.

Stress, anxiety and depression in young people (and in staff)

Looking at the evidence that is out there, it appears that many of our young people and teachers are stressed and unhappy, and something needs to be done about this. According to *The Good Childhood Report 2016*, ten per cent of the children surveyed said they were 'languishing' with low levels of wellbeing and poor mental health (The Children's Society, 2016). Another report cites similar findings, stating that around three children in every class will experience mental health issues between the ages of five and 16 (Green et al., 2005). A recent article published in *The Guardian*, with data gathered from NHS England, showed a 12 per cent increase in the number of children taking antidepressants between 2015 and 2016 (Marsh, 2017). Indeed, the number of 15- and 16-year-olds with depression has nearly doubled between the 1980s and 2000s (Nuffield Foundation, 2012).

The picture doesn't look that much brighter for teachers either, with one survey showing that 67 per cent of the 3,500 teachers surveyed felt that teaching had negatively impacted their mental or physical health, and over 50 per cent had seen a doctor due to stress (NASUWT, 2016). In her book, *How To Survive In Teaching*, Dr Emma Kell's research shows that 57 per cent of the teachers surveyed would '*not* recommend teaching to a close friend or relative.' (Kell, 2018) The teaching profession in the UK also has an alarming dropout rate with almost a third of teachers leaving the profession within the first five years of qualifying, according to government figures (Weale, 2016). Teacher stress is bad for pupils too because burnt-out teachers can't teach and care for them as well as they might and so this in itself means pupil attainment falls (Black, 2001).

I believe a lot of the stress pupils and teachers face in schools is unnecessary and it comes from them lacking autonomy and not seeing the purpose of what they are doing. By focusing more on the happiness and wellbeing of pupils and teaching staff, schools can be a force for good, preventing the decline in children's mental health, reversing the dropout rate of teachers and restoring teaching to a noble, meaningful and deeply satisfying profession.

The purpose of education and the purpose of life

When you ask parents what they want most for their children, more often than not they will answer along the lines of, 'I want them to be happy.' And, if you think about it, we as adults too want the same thing for ourselves. In fact, all humans want to be happy. Regardless of race, gender, age, or any other distinguishing factor, all people are striving for that aim. British philosopher David Hume (1826) argued that 'the great end of all human industry is the attainment of happiness. For this were arts invented, sciences cultivated, laws ordained, and societies modelled.' (p. 167)

So, if happiness is the thing we all want, and we know that we can learn to be happier, it follows that schools should help to teach children the skills to live a happy life. Shouldn't this goal, above all else, be the purpose of education? A child's happiness is bigger and more important than just their academic grades. Research backs this up. One longitudinal study led by Lord Richard Layard at the London School of Economics tracked people from childhood through to adulthood. The study wanted to work out what the best predictors were in childhood of adult happiness. The study concluded that 'the most powerful childhood predictor of adult life-satisfaction is the child's emotional health…The least powerful predictor is the child's intellectual development.' (Layard et al., 2013) In essence, the grades a child gets at school do not predict a happy life. Similarly, PISA (the Programme for International Student Assessment – a worldwide study by the Organisation for Economic Co-operation and Development of 15-year-old school pupils' performance on mathematics, science and reading), who have started to gather data on student wellbeing for the first time, found that 'top-performing students are only slightly more satisfied with their life than students who perform at an average level. There is no clear relationship between study time and life satisfaction.' (OECD, 2017)

But, if children's emotional health is key to them growing up to be happy adults, can primary schools and teachers actually influence this crucial aspect of their lives? The answer is a resounding, yes! In his book, *The Origins of Happiness*, Layard and his colleagues present the evidence that shows that, 'Primary and secondary schools have *major* effects on the emotional wellbeing of their children... These effects of primary schools and teachers persist throughout the following five years and longer.' (Clark et al., 2018)

I believe that our education system has been barking up the wrong tree for many years. With our singular obsession with academic performance data, we have lost sight of what education should really be for, and are squeezing much of the meaning and pleasure from our schools. By teaching happiness and wellbeing at school, we teach children how to: love learning; focus and work hard; look after themselves and the people around them; deal with life's difficulties; and reach their full potential. This in turn adds a greater sense of meaning and purpose to teaching and so enhances teacher wellbeing too.

Positive education – a new era

There appears to be the beginning of a shift in our education system right now. Children, teachers and parents are calling for wellbeing to be at the heart of schools, more and more. People are beginning to wake up to the damage that a relentless focus on exams and academic performance does to our children. A new model for education called positive education is emerging. The positive education movement argues that you can have both academic attainment *and* wellbeing in schools and that they are not mutually exclusive. The International Positive Education Network (IPEN) is one organisation attempting to bring together teachers, pupils, parents and academics to promote positive education, reform the education system and change government policy. The chief medical officer of England makes the case for positive education very clear: 'promoting physical and mental health in schools creates a virtuous circle reinforcing children's attainment and achievement that in turn improves their wellbeing, enabling children to thrive and achieve their full potential.' (Public Health England, 2014) Positive education really is a no-brainer.

How to use this book

Each chapter of this book takes a concept from fields such as positive psychology, behavioural science or neuroscience and breaks it down into two sections: 'In theory' and 'In action'.

In theory shares with you the latest scientific research and evidence behind the concept. It will show how it impacts on people's happiness and wellbeing levels. This section answers the question, 'Why should I do this?' and also gives you, should you need it, evidence to show to headteachers or governors to convince them that trying these ideas is a good thing to do.

In action gives you practical ways that you can bring the theoretical ideas to life in a primary classroom. Many of the practical ideas have come from my own teaching practice but some have come from other teachers. This section answers the question, 'How can I do this?' As you read this section, it is worth reflecting on how you could apply the lessons to your own life as well. I also share some real-life stories in the 'Tales from the classroom' sections but all names have been changed to protect the identity of the children involved.

You can choose to read this book from start to finish, or if a particular idea or theme appeals to you, feel free to jump to that section of the book and try out some of the ideas in your classroom. Chapters 4, 5 and 6 (pp. 61–110) are best read together though, as they all deal with the theme of teaching children how they learn and how best to achieve their full potential.

As with any new ideas for the classroom, you may need to tweak them to suit your children, and also give them time to embed. For example, don't expect to see immediate and dramatic results when you first start to incorporate mindfulness meditation into your daily routine. Give yourself and the children time to get to know the activities, and be patient. Most of all, approach any changes you introduce with an attitude of experimentation and curiosity. In the 'Further reading and recommended resources' section of the book (pp. 181–8), I give some guidance on how you can attempt to measure pupil and staff wellbeing in your school. Not only is this useful data to collect, but also it can help you measure the impact of the interventions you have introduced in your class.

The aim of this book is to equip primary school staff with the knowledge and ideas to start to put wellbeing at the heart of their classrooms, and also to inspire them to take action. As Tal Ben-Shahar's quote at the start of this chapter notes, if you want children to lead happier lives, you first must believe that happiness is the most important thing there is (or the 'ultimate currency' as Ben-Shahar calls it). We can either wait for our education system to change, or we can begin to positively change it ourselves from the ground up. Who knows what may happen as a result?

Chapter 1
Creating a tribal classroom

Alone we can do so little. Together we can do so much.

– Helen Keller

Chapter overview

In this chapter, we explore the work of psychology professor, Louis Cozolino, who created the concept of the 'tribal classroom'. When we tap into our pupils' primitive social instincts, he argues, it can have powerful effects on their wellbeing and ability to learn.

In theory	In action
• Understand our tribal roots	• Design a team flag
• The tribal classroom	• Greetings and endings
• The social brain	• Teaching social skills
• Attachment-based teaching	• Humour and games
• Positive relationships	• Residential and outdoor trips

In theory

Understand our tribal roots

Before we look at what tribal classrooms are, we need to understand more about our tribal history. According to Louis Cozolino, as a species, human beings really haven't had enough time to evolve and move away from our tribal past (Cozolino, 2013). For the majority of the last 100,000 years, it is thought that modern humans lived in hunter-gatherer tribes of between 50 and 75 individuals. These small communities would forage for food and resources and they were held together by family relationships, rituals and the need to cooperate in order to survive (Richerson and Boyd, 1998). Tribal groups were small, based on the values of cooperation, equality, fairness and cohesiveness, decision-making was democratic and there were shared responsibilities. More recently, in the last 5,000 years, Western culture has moved from tribal- to agricultural- to industrial-based societies. It may seem that 5,000 years is a very long period of time but in terms of biological evolution it is a nanosecond.

In our modern industrialised societies, we tend to live in larger groups (in towns and cities), our society is based more on values like individualism and competition, and there tends to be more of a hierarchy and imposed rules. Cozolino believes that our modern cultures often clash with, and are mismatched to, our basic social instincts and even our neurobiology and that this causes us stress, anxiety and unhappiness.

At our core, we are a tribal species and we function best and are happiest when we live and work in tribes. By creating tribal classrooms, we are able to fulfil some of our pupils' core physical and emotional needs. Therefore, Cozolino states that, 'Teachers who are able to tap into the primitive social instincts of their students through attachment relationships and build tribal classrooms succeed in seemingly impossible educational situations.' (Cozolino, 2013, p. xxiv) Children's brains literally get turned on when they feel part of a tribal classroom.

The tribal classroom

But what exactly is a tribal classroom? Well, Cozolino believes a tribal classroom would embody tribal qualities such as democratic leadership, cooperation, teamwork, equality, fairness, trust and strong personal relationships. In a tribe, everyone feels valued and has a role to play. A tribe is essentially a big family and if we can create this atmosphere in our classrooms, children can really begin to flourish. Cozolino explains that, 'Tribal teachers become loving and protective parents to their pupils, who in turn become caring and supportive siblings to one another.' (Cozolino, 2013, p. 245) This familial environment would be full of positive relationships that foster secure attachments between teacher and pupil, which in turn promote the release of the bonding hormone and neurotransmitter, oxytocin (more on this later, p. 16). Therefore, teachers are central to establishing a tribal classroom environment. You would be like a tribal elder – wise, experienced, brave and fair. Your job is to help your children feel like they belong. Research shows that a sense of belonging at school is fundamental to learning (Ryan and Powelson, 1991). And when children feel that they belong, then they will feel safe to explore and take risks.

Many of the pupils we teach have incredibly stressful home lives, so tribal classrooms purposefully create a calm, safe environment. Ridicule and shame have no place in a tribal classroom but humour and light-heartedness do. Teachers who can incorporate appropriate humour into their teaching practice can counteract the inevitable stress and tension of our education system. Tribal classrooms also include a lot of play. Research has shown that exploration and play are a core part of our natural learning and are essential to neuroplasticity (the ability of our brain to grow and change). Play activates the release of other 'happy hormones', such as dopamine, serotonin and endorphins, which boost feelings of wellbeing, aid learning and foster social connectivity (Cozolino, 2013, pp. 171–2).

Finally, stories and storytelling are a core feature of tribal classrooms. Storytelling is woven into the fabric of our nature and has a deep evolutionary history. The role of storytelling in tribes was for memory storage, emotional regulation and social cohesion (Cozolino, 2013, p. 187). Clearly, storytelling has as much relevance for children today as it did for our ancestors. Stories enrich children's emotional vocabulary and allow them to learn from a character's moral dilemmas. In the writing and telling of their own stories, children also get to express themselves and better understand the world around them.

The social brain

It is a widely held view among psychologists and neuroscientists that humans possess a social brain. What this means is that our brains are shaped and sculpted significantly by our nurture and social relationships. In fact, there are certain parts of the brain, like the amygdala (see Chapter 2, p. 31 and Chapter 3, p. 46), that have neurons in them that will only fire in response to other people's reactions (Ratey, 2003, pp. 295–6). Additionally, the discovery of mirror neurons by neurophysiologist, Giacomo Rizzolatti, also supports the idea of the social brain. Mirror neurons fire when we carry out an action, or witness someone else carry out an action and they might move us to imitate what we observe. Mirror neurons are also thought to be partly responsible for our ability to empathise with other people and feel what they are feeling. For example, when someone else laughs at a joke, even if we haven't heard the joke, we feel the urge to laugh too. Or if someone bangs their head, we might grab *our* heads and go 'Ouch!'. It is clear that our brains change in response to other people and our interactions with them.

Looking further into our evolutionary past, we begin to see why. As primates began to live in increasingly larger social groups, their brains started to get larger and more complex. These larger social groups were able to provide more dedicated childcare, stimulation and challenge to the brain, which supported its growth further (Dunbar, 1992). This laid the foundations for the development of our language, problem-solving skills and complex thinking abilities. The brains humans have today have been grown and moulded over hundreds of thousands of years by the social groups and tribes they were raised in.

The implication of all of this is that *how* we look after the children in our care will have a far bigger impact on their development than anything we explicitly teach them. Psychology professor, Alison Gopnik, goes as far as saying, 'Children actually learn more from the unconscious details of what caregivers do than from any of the conscious manipulations' (Gopnik, 2016, p. 90). In starting to design your tribal classroom, it is important to bear in mind that we need to give the children in our care something good to imitate and that the atmosphere in your tribe is crucial for their brain development and wellbeing. As tribal leaders, teachers can have a significant impact on their tribe's lives.

Attachment-based teaching

Psychologists call love 'attachment', I guess because it sounds less problematic than 'love' and is maybe easier to measure. Either way, attachment psychologists study how young children feel about their caregivers (normally mothers in these experiments) and one way they do this is by separating one-year-olds from their caregivers, whilst leaving them in a room with a stranger, and then reuniting them. Generally, the children will fall into one of the following four categories of attachment:

1. securely attached
2. avoidantly attached
3. anxiously attached
4. disorganised attached.

The 'secure' children will show distress when their caregiver leaves and joy when they return. The 'avoidant' children look away when their caregiver leaves and appear ambivalent even when they return. 'Anxious' children get very distressed when separated and then continue to be inconsolable when reunited. 'Disorganised' children will often display strange behaviour like spinning around in circles or collapsing to the ground. These children often have parents who display frightened or frightening behaviour to their children and, as a result, the inner turmoil in the child causes their coping skills and even motor skills to become disorganised. Also, the worrying thing noted by psychologists about 'avoidant' children, who on the surface seem fine and not really bothered when left alone, is that when their heart rates are monitored they are actually very upset but have learned to hide their true feelings.

Attachment styles are important because they affect children's wellbeing, their ability to learn and their behaviour. They tend to follow us into adulthood too and shape our future relationships. The behaviour of insecurely attached children can often be the expression of anxiety and fear. So, what looks like disobedience and 'bad' behaviour on the surface may actually be their way of coping with difficult feelings and an inability to regulate their emotions (Cozolino, 2013, p. 57). Our classrooms will be full of an array of children (and teachers) with varying attachment styles, but the good news is that tribal teachers and classrooms can create a secure base for all children so they feel supported and safe. Cozolino says that, 'Children learn best when they feel protected and connected. The goal of attachment-based teaching is to have each child move from feeling vulnerable, frightened and unimportant to feeling protected, cared for and valued – a state…that optimises learning.' (Cozolino, 2013, p. 241) Tribal classrooms are essential for promoting secure attachments among its pupils because they foster strong, positive relationships where children feel safe and cared for.

Positive relationships

Ultimately, creating a tribal classroom is about establishing and investing in positive relationships between the teaching adults and the children, and between the children themselves. These are relationships based on trust, honesty, support, kindness, love, friendship and teamwork. Positive relationships have been a core part of our survival as a species and the backbone of tribes. Writing in the late 19th century about human evolution, Charles Darwin stated that, 'Those communities which included the greatest number of the most sympathetic members would flourish best, and rear the greatest number of offspring' (Darwin, 1871). To foster positive relationships, we need to be mindful about how much criticism we give children in relation to the amount of praise we give them. Studies by relationship expert John Gottman show that successful relationships have an average ratio of 5:1 in terms of positive to negative interactions (Gottman, 1994). The Institute of Child Education and Psychology (ICEP) notes that, for children, this ratio should probably be even higher for them to flourish and we should aim for about seven or eight positive interactions for every negative one (ICEP, Module 2, p. 13).

Not only do positive relationships aid survival in our species, but they also positively impact our health and even help us to live longer. Studies show that just being around supportive others can have a huge impact on our health and can reduce blood pressure, stress hormones and the risk of getting ill (Cozolino, 2013, p. 112). Positive relationships also promote the release of the 'happy hormone' oxytocin in our brains. Oxytocin is often called the 'love' or 'tend and befriend' hormone and is fundamental in creating secure attachments between children and their caregivers. Mothers' bodies are flooded with oxytocin when they give birth as it helps them bond with their newborn babies, and is necessary for the production of breast milk. It promotes feelings of trust and empathy, and has been shown to reduce levels of anxiety. People who are administered oxytocin seem to be more trusting and it makes them more willing to share and cooperate (Gopnik, 2016, p. 70). There is no doubt that positive relationships would have been key in the development of our social brain and in the survival of our tribal ancestors, and they are crucial for tribal classrooms today.

In action

I am certain that many great teachers naturally create tribal classrooms without even realising that this is what they are doing. It is instinctive for these teachers to create tribal classrooms for the very reason that it is woven into our DNA. It just feels right and natural to create a sense of family in your classroom. Taking Cozolino's messages on board, here are a few ways that you can create a tribal classroom in your school.

Design a team flag

Developing a sense of team in your class can be a great way to bring out children's tribal instincts. Here's how you could do this by creating a team flag:

- At the beginning of a school year, get your new class to think about what makes a good team (this is your version of a tribe). Discuss some ideas and then show a video montage of one of the most successful teams around – Team GB. The great thing about Team GB is that it is full of inspiring role models from both genders and is culturally diverse.

- After watching a highly emotive Team GB montage (there are quite a few on **www.youtube.com** but this is my favourite: **www.youtube.com/watch?v=gKJDjg4ebNQ**), brainstorm the qualities and values that a good team needs. Typically, the children come up with ideas like 'teamwork', 'friendship', 'kindness', 'effort', 'love', 'trust', 'honesty', 'perseverance' and 'resilience'.

- Scribe these on the board as the children call them out. Then tell your class that, like Team GB, they are a team. 'We are now Team XXXX,' I normally proclaim proudly. (Team Year 4 Green, Team Year 2, Team Picasso, Team Monet are some of my previous teams).

- Tell them that any great team needs a team flag and that they are going to make their own. Then ask each child to choose one value from the board that really means something to them and to write it in bold on a piece of paper, and fill their page with colour and patterns. You want this to be as eye-catching as possible as this is your team flag and it represents who you are!

- It really doesn't matter if more than one child writes 'love', or 'teamwork' but I do try to encourage children to choose something else they like if I can see too many instances of 'kindness' in the room (not that you can ever have too much kindness, of course). Once each child has finished their part of the flag, piece all of the parts together and you have one large, eye-catching, unique team flag! (See Figure 1.1 below for an example.)

Now, the flag is just the beginning, but it represents the values of your new team and family and gives your tribe a sense of identity. When I teach, I will constantly refer to our flag and our team. Every time I want my class's attention, I'll say, 'Right, Team Monet, listen up!' I do this to remind each team member that they are part of something bigger than themselves, and that they belong. The flag stays up throughout the year on display in our class as a symbol of our values and that every member has a part to play in the success of our team.

Figure 1.1: Team Year 4's flag

Tales from the classroom

It was early August and I already had 'the fear' about the new class I was inheriting in September. Year 2 had been a handful for their previous two teachers. So much so that their Reception and Year 1 teachers had both had time off for stress when they had been teaching them. I can remember my first week with Year 2 – I was constantly barking instructions and dishing out sanctions. My positive behaviour management had gone out of the window! They just weren't gelling as a class. There was no cohesion, no sense of cooperation. At every opportunity, they would tell on each other and try to get one another into trouble. Fortunately, it was September 2012 and we had just seen the dazzling display of brilliance and teamwork from Team GB at the London 2012 Olympics. Year 2 were the first class I made a team flag with. We discussed at length what qualities Team GB showed at the Olympics, and we designed our class flag around the values we wanted to display in our team. In an instant, we had become *Team Year 2* and we worked hard that year to work better as a team. It certainly wasn't easy, and there were many times where I thought that we'd never make a good team. But, bit by bit, little by little, arguments started to get resolved more quickly. The tale-telling started to wane. The children were more likely to share and take turns. They started being kinder to each other and supporting one another. By the end of that year, and it was one of the longest years of my teaching career (an Ofsted inspection fell slap bang in the middle of it!), I was completely besotted with Team Year 2. I was lucky enough to get them back when I moved into Year 4. We continued to work on our teamwork and we had become a proper little tribal family by the end of Year 4 – arguably a somewhat dysfunctional family, but a family nonetheless. I left the school that year but two years later returned just to attend that class's leavers' assembly in Year 6. It's amazing what a class flag and a bit of teamwork can do.

Greetings and endings

If we're trying to establish a sense of family in our tribal classrooms, I feel it is really important that all of your pupils experience a warm and positive greeting in the morning and a fond farewell at the end of the day. Why not try these ideas when greeting your class in the morning?

- Greet your pupils at the door of the classroom with a smile and by saying their name. Not only are smiles contagious, so it is an easy way to spread some positivity throughout your tribe at the start of the day, but it signals to the children that they are safe and that you can be trusted. Using their first name is a powerful way of connecting with individual tribe members and signals to them that they have been noticed and that they matter.

- You can mix your greetings up with a handshake, a 'high-five' or a 'fist-bump' as the power of touch can be really important (you work in a primary school so you're allowed to have fun with your tribe!). Remember the happy hormone, oxytocin? Well, it can be released when people touch hands together, so greeting your pupils this way can release the hormone that helps them feel calm, secure and connected. A positive greeting in the morning sets the tone for the rest of the day.

Endings are crucial too, especially when the day has been difficult for some of your tribe. If people's days end on a negative, even if it was largely positive overall, they will generally rate it and remember it as a bad day. Conversely, 'peak-end' theory demonstrates that if endings are positive, people will rate the overall experience as positive even if, on average, the experience was poor (Kahneman et al., 1993). So try to end your day positively by experimenting with these ideas:

- End your day reading a chapter or two from a great story. Nothing conjures up an image of a tribe more than being gathered round a camp fire listening to tales of the past, so always bring your class together for a story. It's great when a chapter ends with a cliffhanger, as your tribe will be desperate to find out what happens next and will look forward to story time again with anticipation!

- You could play live music videos or a funny Michael Rosen performance poem to end the day – just to get their positive emotions pumping and to end the day on a high.

- If one of your tribe has not had such a great day in terms of their behaviour, it is really important to remind them of the team flag and the values they are expected to uphold but also that tomorrow is a new day and a fresh start. Putting your arm around their shoulder and reminding them of the positive choices they had made in the day reinforces that you care about them, that their day was not entirely bad, and that you have high expectations of them that you know they can rise to. This allows you to maintain boundaries but you're doing it in a positive way.

Teaching social skills

There will be children in your tribe who regularly make poor choices and who find it difficult to fit in. The most important thing for these children is not to give up on them. Yes, they will take up most of your time. Yes, they will push your buttons. And yes, they will keep making the same mistakes despite pep talks, encouragement and constant reminders about making the right choices. But, as the saying goes, 'the children who need the most love, will ask for it in the most unloving ways.' Often, these children simply have not had the nurture, upbringing or positive role models in their lives to help them develop the social skills to thrive in a tribal classroom. Helping these children find their way and feel part of the tribe will be far more important and useful for their lives than teaching them how to use subordinate clauses. In such circumstances, it has been shown to be beneficial to directly teach social skills to children (Ratey, 2003, p. 299), and you could try these ideas:

- Set aside time each week for your class to play card and board games. All children will learn and practise the skills of taking turns, sharing, listening and responding, as well as how to win and lose graciously. Games are also great for developing cognitive skills, as children have to learn the rules and then develop strategies to win.

- Use drama and role-play to act out different social situations. It could be practising how to politely ask others to join a game in the playground, or how to deal with another child who is being mean to you. When children are put in role-play social situations and then rehearse their different responses, their brains are learning how to handle those situations in the future.

- When reading your class story at the end of the day, be sure to discuss any social situations that characters find themselves in, where they may be experiencing a problem or dilemma. Get your children to put themselves in the characters' shoes and ask, 'What would you do in that situation?' Getting children to see others' perspectives is a key part of developing empathy, a crucial social skill.

Humour and games

Successful tribal classrooms definitely incorporate fun and laughter in an appropriate way into the school day. I think it is important that teachers don't take themselves too seriously and find opportunities to laugh with the children and at themselves. I'm certainly not proposing that you become the class clown and just try to make wisecracks all day, but having a sense of humour shows that you are human, and by sharing laughter with your tribe, you can bring everyone together in an inclusive way. Here are three simple games to play with your class:

- **Call my bluff**: This is one of the best getting-to-know-you games to try at the start of the year. Each child and adult in the classroom writes down two lies about themselves and one truth. The lies shouldn't be too obvious like, 'I once flew to the moon wearing a Donald Trump onesie.' Everyone takes a turn to read out their three personal 'facts' and the teacher has to guess which one is the lie. If the teacher gets it wrong, one point to the class but if they get it correct, one point to the teacher. The children then get to guess their teacher's lie. This game can be really funny and is a great way of finding out more about your tribe. You also get to know who the really good liars are, which can be insightful! You can play this game at various points in the year when it should be harder to hoodwink your tribe as they get to know you even more.

- **Pass the hug**: When teaching a tribe of six-year-olds, I created a game called 'pass the hug'. The children sat in a circle with their eyes closed. I would touch someone on their shoulder and they had to pass a hug to the person next to them. The hug would get passed round until it reached the start person again who then called out 'Stop!'. The children then had to guess who had passed the first hug. Now it's not the most challenging game, but I invented it because

I knew that hugging releases oxytocin, and that the children found it hilarious to hug one another. Seeing the children beaming with smiles anticipating the hug, and then giggling away when someone hugged them was great. The children often asked to play this game. Usually at the start of a maths lesson! It's a nice game to play near the end of a busy week.

- **Bounce buzz**: Another popular game I play with the children is my version of the maths game 'Fizz Buzz'. In 'Bounce buzz', the children stand in a circle and someone starts with a large, soft bouncy ball. As the ball gets passed round the circle, each child says a number in sequence starting from 'one'. When they get to a multiple of five they don't say the number, instead they bounce the ball and say 'bounce', and pass the ball to the next person who carries on with the counting. When they get to a multiple of ten they don't say the number, instead they bounce the ball twice saying, 'bounce buzz'. If you make a mistake (e.g. by not bouncing the ball, or by saying the number instead of 'bounce' or 'bounce buzz') you sit down and are out of this round.

As the children get good at playing this version, start to make the game harder. You can move to passing the ball randomly around the circle (if it's a poor throw, or you drop the ball, you're out). You can then introduce rules like you can't pass to the person next to you, or pass back to the person who just threw to you. You could change the multiples, by using threes and sixes.

You can then move on to 'Super-speed bounce buzz' where the children are given very little time to catch the ball and pass it on to the next person whilst correctly saying the right number or phrase. The game can end when there are, say, five people left in, or it can go down to having a single winner. The great thing about this game is that it is fast, frenetic and fun. It definitely improves children's numerical, throwing, catching and coordination skills. Games like this can even help improve children's working memory, as they have to mentally juggle the numbers, phrases and various rules. Plus, everyone can succeed at this game – the children who win are not always the best mathematicians or throwers and catchers. And if anyone really dominates in this game you can always get them to put their stronger throwing hand behind their back and get them to play one-handed.

Humour and games can be a great way to punctuate your day. They can galvanise a tribe together, raise morale and reduce any stress or tension. I would recommend that all teachers add more of these elements into their teaching practice.

Residential and outdoor trips

Another way to bring the inner tribesman out of you and your class is to go on a residential trip. These trips often involve lots of time spent outdoors in natural settings with various activities, such as canoeing, abseiling, den building, orienteering and team building.

They are a fantastic way to bring your tribe together and push them out of their comfort zones (see Chapter 5, p. 77 for more on this). Not only do the children become more physically active and get back in touch with nature, but they also get to learn in a novel and non-conventional way. The children always learn lots about themselves on these trips and discover talents and inner resources that they never knew they had. I often see sides to my children that I didn't know existed

Figure 1.2: Some of Team Monet on their residential trip

when on residential trips, and it is often the children that struggle academically and behaviourally in class that really shine. Figure 1.2 shows some of Team Monet posing for the camera as they take a break from building their den. I am a big advocate of residential trips and have enjoyed every single one I have been on.

If you don't feel your class is old enough for a residential trip (the youngest age group I have taken away is a class of nine-year-olds), or budgets won't allow it, then a day trip to an outdoor activity centre can be a great alternative. Here the children may get to experience activities like high-rope tree climbing where they navigate round a course with various obstacles in the way (like cargo nets and zip wires). Again, the point is to get children outdoors and back in touch with the hunter-gatherer in them. The shared experience of getting round what can be quite a scary obstacle course will foster the tribal spirit among your team.

Key points

- Humans are an innately tribal species. Our ancestors lived in tribal communities based on familial ties, cooperation and cohesion. We still have our roots firmly planted in our tribal past.

- Tribal classrooms tap into children's primitive social instincts and create safe and secure learning environments where children feel that they belong, and are able to take risks, play and explore. This turns on their brains for learning and fosters wellbeing.

- Create a sense of tribe in your classroom by discussing the values and attributes of good teams and making your own class flag. Work towards becoming a good team.

- Ensure your day starts with a positive greeting and ending. Even if behaviour has been challenging, find ways to address the behaviour that show that you have high expectations and that you care.

- You may need to directly teach social skills to some children but, ultimately, the best teaching comes from modelling the behaviour you wish to see. Your tribe will imitate the example you set as the tribal leader.

- Play more games with your class to galvanise your tribe, inject some fun into your day, and reduce any stress or tension that may arise in the school week.
- Tap into your pupils' inner tribespeople by taking them on an outdoor residential trip, if time and budget permit. At the very least, get them outdoors more and back in touch with nature.

Chapter 2
Mindfulness

If every eight-year-old in the world is taught meditation, we will eliminate violence from the world within one generation.

— His Holiness, the Dalai Lama

Chapter overview

There has recently been an explosion in mindfulness interventions in schools, workplaces and business. But does mindfulness live up to the hype? In this chapter, we will look at what mindfulness is, how it can benefit your pupils, and how you can authentically introduce mindfulness practices into your classroom.

In theory	In action
• Origins of Western mindfulness • What is mindfulness? • Autopilot and mind wandering • Looking inside the brain • The stress response – fight or flight • Anxiety, depression and mindfulness • Children and mindfulness	• Embodying mindfulness • Children's response to mindfulness • Meditating with children • Mindfulness practices

In theory

Origins of Western mindfulness

In Massachusetts Medical School in the late 1970s, a radical doctor named Jon Kabat-Zinn was experimenting with a new way for treating patients who suffered with chronic pain, illness and stress. His patients had largely been failed by modern medicine, which hadn't been able to alleviate their acute suffering. Kabat-Zinn had created an eight-week course, *Mindfulness-Based Stress Reduction (MBSR)*, which involved patients meditating, performing mindful movement exercises and relating to their thoughts, feelings and body sensations in an entirely new way. Surprisingly, the MBSR course had profound positive effects for the patients who were at last able to regain some control of their health and attain some peace of mind. Although mindfulness has its roots in 2,500-year-old Buddhist teachings (and other contemplative traditions of Asia), Kabat-Zinn's MBSR course was entirely secular and it has spawned an explosion of mindfulness-based courses and interventions in the West. One such variation of MBSR, is *Mindfulness-Based Cognitive Therapy (MBCT)* which was developed by three scientists who wanted to help treat people with recurrent depression.

The fact that MBSR and MBCT courses were introduced into Western medicine by doctors and scientists rather than spiritual yogi-type figures (like Transcendental Meditation, for example) might explain why it has been so well received and accepted into mainstream Western culture. MBSR courses are now subject to numerous clinical trials and studies around the world, and the University of Oxford set up the Oxford Mindfulness Centre in 2008, which offers training in and research into mindfulness interventions. The National Institute of Health and Care Excellence in the UK (NICE – a body that advises the NHS on which drugs and interventions to use) recommended MBCT in 2004 to treat people with depression and in 2009, the recommendation was updated and given 'key priority' status. There is even the Mindfulness All-Party Parliamentary Group (MAPPG) in the UK Government, which was set up in 2014 to review the evidence and best practice of mindfulness and how it can affect policy decisions based on its findings. With so much time, effort and money being invested into mindfulness on a national and global scale, there is no doubt that mindfulness interventions are firmly part of mainstream Western culture and that it is here to stay and not just a passing fad.

What is mindfulness?

Mindfulness has become very on-trend in educational settings in recent years and is becoming more mainstream. However, some mindfulness practitioners worry that a 'McMindfulness' culture is taking root and quick fixes are being introduced by teachers who have no proper training or background in mindfulness. Although teachers may be meditating with their classes, they do not know exactly what mindfulness is, the critics argue.

One of the best definitions I have come across that neatly sums up what mindfulness is comes from *Mindful Nation UK* (a report published in 2015 by the MAPPG), which states that:

> *'Mindfulness means paying attention to what's happening in the present moment in the mind, body and external environment, with an attitude of curiosity and kindness. It is typically cultivated by a range of simple meditation practices, which aim to bring a greater awareness of thinking, feeling and behaviour patterns, and to develop the capacity to manage these with greater skill and compassion. This is found to lead to an expansion of choice and capacity in how to meet and respond to life's challenges, and therefore live with greater wellbeing, mental clarity and care for yourself and others.' (MAPPG, 2015, p. 13)*

So, in its simplest form, mindfulness is about being aware of what is happening in the here and now. To 'be mindful' according to Rick Hanson, means 'Having good control over your attention: you can place your attention wherever you want and it stays there; when you want to shift it to something else, you can.' (Hanson, 2009, p. 177) Now, this may sound very simple, but the fact is our minds do not just stay where we want them to. They drag up memories from the past, or they fast-forward to the future and, often, we do not take in what is happening right now. Therefore, mindfulness can also be seen as a type of mind training, which strengthens the attentional- and emotional-regulating parts of the brain.

Autopilot and mind wandering

Our minds have an amazing ability to automate many parts of our lives using habits. If we did not have this ability to learn from repetition, we'd still be trying to remember how to dress ourselves every time we woke up in the morning. When we operate on 'autopilot' it means we can do things automatically, like driving our cars or eating our food, with our minds free to think about other things (like that lesson after break that we haven't planned yet!). But, over time, we can give over too much control to autopilot and we can end up living most of our lives without full awareness of what we are doing. We can miss a lot of life's richness and many small moments, like the smile of a grateful pupil or a reassuringly warm summer breeze, can simply pass us by.

When operating on autopilot, we often enter a state known as 'mind wandering' – with our minds not focused on what we are doing. Two psychologists at Harvard University, Matthew Killingsworth and Daniel Gilbert, discovered that, on average, people spend about 47 per cent of their waking hours in a mind-wandering state (Killingsworth and Gilbert, 2010). More importantly, they found that this mind wandering depletes us and lowers our levels of happiness: 'A human mind is a wandering mind and a wandering mind is an unhappy mind.' (Killingsworth and Gilbert, 2010). Numerous studies have shown that mindfulness meditation is an antidote to this mind–wandering malaise. By strengthening certain parts of the brain, mindfulness helps bring us back into the present moment more often and gives us greater control over our attention.

Looking inside the brain

One of the most interesting discoveries about mindfulness is how it can physically change our brains. With the benefit of MRI scanners and EEG machines, neuroscientists are able to track what happens inside the brain when people take part in mindful meditation practices. One of the leading neuroscientists in this field is Professor Richard Davidson. By spying inside our brains, Davidson found that when people were angry, upset, worried or depressed, an area of the brain known as the right pre-frontal cortex lights up (the neurons in this part of the brain are firing away). However, when people are in a positive mood, joyful, enthusiastic and upbeat, Davidson saw that there was more neural activity in the left pre-frontal cortex (Davidson, 2004).

Davidson and Kabat-Zinn teamed up to monitor what might happen to a group of biotech workers' brains after they had taken part in an eight-week MBSR course (Davidson et al., 2003). Amazingly, there had been a significant shift of brain activity towards the left pre-frontal cortex so these workers reported feeling happier and far less stressed than the control group. Another unexpected consequence of the MBSR course was that the workers' immune systems became significantly stronger too – they had more antibodies in their blood when given a flu jab, compared to the control group.

The stress response – fight or flight

A tiny yet extremely powerful part of the brain, known as the amygdala, is often behind a lot of our stress and unhappiness. When we sense a threat, or we're fearful or anxious about something, the amygdala kicks in and prepares us to either fight the threat, or run away from it. The amygdala is a 'primeval' part of our brain and would have been crucial for keeping us alive during our hunter-gatherer days (see Chapter 3, p. 46), but it also means it can be very simplistic in how it interprets danger. For example, it makes no distinction whatsoever between a real threat, like a dangerous dog trying to attack you, or an imagined threat, like the thought about a looming deadline. It treats both scenarios in exactly the same way and prepares your body for the stress response, often referred to as 'fight or flight'.

The stress response broadly works as follows: a threat is sensed by the amygdala and it sends signals to other parts of the body to prepare for 'fight or flight'. Our heart rate increases to pump more blood and oxygen to our muscles. The adrenal glands release the stress hormone cortisol into our blood stream. Cortisol makes you hyper vigilant, it halts your immune system, stops your ability to learn and prevents you from relaxing. According to psychotherapist, Sue Gerhardt, it is as if cortisol is having the following conversation with other bodily systems: 'Stop what you're doing, guys! This is an emergency! Don't waste time fighting bugs. Don't waste time learning or connecting new pathways. Don't relax! I want all your attention on this problem!' (Gerhardt, 2014, pp. 61–2) This works brilliantly when the threat is real, and it enables us to escape from it and, therefore, to survive. Once the threat has passed, our bodies can return to normal – the extra cortisol is reabsorbed into the body, our heart rate slows back down and we can think clearly again. Except that this doesn't always happen. If we continue to feel stressed or threatened, the stress response keeps working and cortisol stays in our system. If too much cortisol is released, or when it is released unnecessarily, it can cause damage to our brains and bodies, even killing brain cells (Davidson and Begley, 2012, p. 120).

You can see how the everyday stresses of home and school life can mean that many of our pupils may be operating on a kind of 'fight or flight' basis for a lot of their lives. Imagine a pupil who hasn't done their homework and thinks they will get in trouble. Or a pupil about to sit a maths test who feels unprepared and worried about failing. The amygdala will be firing away with these threats, even though they are not life-threatening. Over time, if we stay in this hyper-vigilant state of arousal, it can deplete us. We start to get ill more frequently, we struggle to learn as well and we can start to feel that we don't have the inner resources for the challenges of our lives. If we're not careful, we can end up suffering periods of acute anxiety and depression.

Anxiety, depression and mindfulness

But it is not all doom and gloom. More and more studies are showing that mindfulness can really help us cope with the increased stresses of daily life.

In the UK, one of the leading experts in mindfulness-based interventions is Professor Mark Williams. Williams was one of the three scientists who adapted Kabat-Zinn's MBSR course and created MBCT to help patients who suffer with anxiety and depression. Williams and his colleagues have found that MBCT can significantly reduce the chances of suffering depression (Williams and Penman, 2011). Impressively, it reduces the chance of a relapse by about 40 to 50 per cent in people who have experienced three or more previous episodes of depression. Another study showed that people who came off their antidepressants and did an eight-week MBCT course instead, did as well or better than those who stayed on their medication.

Why does mindfulness have such a positive effect on levels of stress, anxiety and depression? Well, it has a lot to do with the physical changes that take place in the brain when you meditate regularly. As we discovered earlier, there is a shift in brain activity away from a part of the brain that processes negative thoughts and emotions. If our thoughts can be a trigger for the stress response, and if we are having fewer negative or worrying thoughts, then we will not be reacting in the 'fight or flight' mode so much. Davidson also believes that mindfulness can create new neuronal pathways in the brain that change how we respond to stress, so that when we experience a stressful situation, it will get processed in our frontal cortex but fewer of the signals will reach our amygdala (Davidson and Begley, 2012, p. 204). In fact, studies have shown that there is less overall activity in the amygdala in experienced meditators. Over time this boosts our levels of resilience and our ability to cope with stress, rather than being overwhelmed by it.

And mindfulness interventions in schools could not come at a more pressing time. Some educational commentators talk about a 'mental health crisis' in UK schools, citing evidence that half of all mental health problems manifest by the age of 14, with 75 per cent by age 24 (Kessler et al., 2005). Maybe mindfulness in schools could be one of the solutions to this growing problem.

Children and mindfulness

There is one big caveat to the research above, and that is that it was all performed on adults and not on children. But there is a growing body of research and evidence showing the positive effects of mindfulness on young people in line with the adult evidence.

One study looked at the impact of an eight-week MBSR course on 102 children aged four to 18 with a wide range of mental health issues, and they reported significantly reduced symptoms of anxiety, depression and distress, and increased self-esteem and better-quality sleep. At a three-month follow-up, the pupils who practised the most showed improved levels of anxiety and depression compared to those who did not (MAPPG, 2015, p. 30). With mindfulness, the adage 'practice makes progress' holds true. Another study by Professor Willem Kuyken in 2013 reported that teenagers who had completed a mindfulness intervention course (the .b curriculum created by the Mindfulness in Schools Project) had significantly lower levels of depressive symptoms, stress and greater wellbeing (Kuyken et al., 2013).

Alongside this, cognitive neuroscientist Dusana Dorjee at Bangor University is currently studying the impact of a mindfulness course for primary school children (the *Paws.b curriculum* created by the Mindfulness in Schools Project). Dorjee's initial findings show that a mindfulness intervention at primary school can significantly reduce negative emotions and improve meta-cognition (i.e. higher-order thinking skills or the ability to be aware of your own thoughts) (Vickery and Dorjee, 2016). Indeed, I took part in a mindfulness research project at the primary school I teach in. Portsmouth University psychology undergraduate, Emily Main, conducted the research, which showed a significant positive correlation between a mindfulness intervention and increased emotional self-regulation, compared to the control group (Main, 2017).

At present, the research into the effects of mindfulness training on children is an emerging field. But the field is growing and more research is being carried out by some of the world's leading universities. Kuyken and Williams at the University of Oxford are two of the lead investigators of the MYRIAD project, which is a six-year study into the effects of a mindfulness training programme on adolescents. It is the largest randomised control study ever undertaken to measure the effects of mindfulness on children's mental health. I look forward to the outcome of that project but, in the meantime, the emergent evidence is promising.

In action

Good teachers have always incorporated 'quiet' times during their day, so children have a chance to be still and reflect. But as primary education has become more pressurised and exam-focused over the years, this 'quiet time' can easily become lost as schools view it as lost 'learning' time. Below I give some practical ways to incorporate more stillness and mindfulness into your school day to support children's learning and emotional wellbeing.

Embodying mindfulness

The best way to incorporate mindfulness into your classroom is to establish your own personal mindfulness practice. My first experience of mindfulness was during my first year of teaching. This was an incredibly stressful time for me – not only was I juggling the demands of university projects and deadlines, but I was also teaching a very lively group of ten-year-olds and, if I'm perfectly honest, I didn't have a clue what I was doing! So, I undertook a four-week online mindfulness course (**www.bemindful.co.uk**) run by the Mental Health Foundation UK. At the start of the course, I had to take a stress test and scored 21 out of 40. My stress levels were slightly below the average, which was 23 out of 40. I couldn't believe that my stress levels were deemed average – I was struggling to sleep at night, my appetite had gone and I dreaded going into school most days! But, according to Mark Williams, stress levels that were deemed 'chronic' in the 1950s are deemed 'average' now. Sadly, to be chronically stressed is now the norm.

However, as I was to discover, the mindfulness course dramatically changed my relationship to my stress. I followed the programme (which was a condensed version of an eight-week MBSR course) and meditated daily, performed body scans and mindful movement exercises (a body scan is where you slowly scan through various parts of your body, bringing your full attention to each part, and you notice what sensations are there; mindful movement exercises are normally based on hatha yoga practices – you move slowly and deliberately, bringing your full attention to your body as it moves) and sometimes kept a record of the positive and negative thoughts and feelings I was having. By the time I had completed the course, I was invited to take

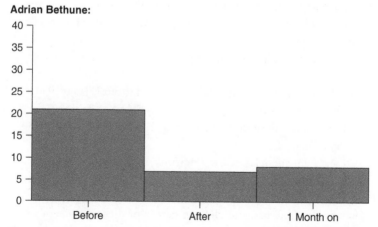

Figure 2.1: A graph showing a dramatic fall in my stress levels after completing my mindfulness course. Reproduced with kind permission from Wellmind Media

the stress test again and my stress levels had dropped by an impressive 66 per cent (see Figure 2.1). I was also sleeping better at night, my appetite had returned and, best of all, I was enjoying teaching and felt happier.

So, my advice to teachers is to give mindfulness a go yourselves. You have nothing to lose. There is also the little matter of authenticity. You cannot hope to cultivate a greater sense of awareness and calm in your class if you are flapping around wildly at school, stressed out of your mind. Claire Kelly, Director at the Mindfulness in Schools Project, puts it well when she says, 'If you are not living the mindfulness principles yourself, the kids will know. If you teach them a lovely mindfulness lesson and then go and kick the photocopier in the corridor, they will notice.' (Jenkin, 2014)

Children's response to mindfulness

From my experience of meditating with children, the response from them and their parents has been overwhelmingly positive. Here is some of the feedback from the children I have taught:

'I feel relaxed and that I'm not going to get into trouble.'
Mojeed, 6
'I feel really good because I relax my brain.' Nancy, 7
'I feel happy because it calms me down.' Dexter, 6
'I like it because I'm normally sleepy in the morning but it wakes me up.' Lara, 7
'Mindfulness helps me when I get nervous or when I can't sleep.'
Olivia, 9
'Whenever I meditate my day is calm, and so am I.' Jamie, 9
'I love meditation, it helps me do my work.' Lucy, 8
'It helps me a great deal when I struggle with my work and at home.' Zak, 9
'I feel calm and relaxed, like I don't have a worry in the world.'
William, 9

You may also find that your children start to meditate outside of school as well. I have had many children tell me that they meditate at night to help them get to sleep. I often hear from parents too, who tell me

Figure 2.2: Children pause mid-lesson for a moment of mindfulness

about the positive difference they notice in their children once they have started meditating.

This doesn't mean that every child will love it. In one class I surveyed, three children said they found it 'boring' and that they didn't like it. However, I would argue that given that moods are contagious, if the 27 other children in my class are meditating and cultivating a peaceful state of mind, then everyone in the class gets to benefit, whether they choose to join in or not. It is such a great way to start the day and can be used at various points throughout the day as well (Figure 2.2 above shows children taking a 'mindful moment' mid-lesson).

Tales from the classroom

When I met Philip for the first time I could see he was a nervous child. I remember the first time I asked him a question during a lesson and could see the panic in his eyes. I knew that he knew the answer but he couldn't find the words to explain it to me. He took to meditation straight away though. It was the part of the day where he could just be. No tests to pass, no right or wrong

---

answers. Just being with his breath. He would often ask me questions about meditation when I was on playground duty. 'Why did you start to meditate? When do you meditate at home?' Philip asked. 'To help me cope with stress and first thing in the morning after my alarm goes off,' I answered. Philip had a keen interest in meditation and I could tell it resonated with him. Then one day, I received an email from his mum:

> 'Philip has embraced mindfulness in a way I can't explain. He absolutely loves it! I've even had lessons from him with extremely detailed explanations of what to do and why. Thank you, Mr Bethune, for introducing this wonderful technique. Philip, believe it or not, is an extremely anxious boy. Meditation is changing his life. It's giving him self-confidence, a focus and the ability to express himself in a way he never could before. Philip has embraced meditation so much so he has asked for a meditation singing bowl for Christmas.'

One time, whilst on playground duty, I asked Philip why he started to meditate and when he does it at home. 'Because you made me, and last thing at night to help me get to sleep,' he answered with a cheeky smile.

Meditating with children

I think it is quite important for any adult guiding meditation practices for the first time to have realistic expectations. Your children may fidget and squirm and be distracted, and that's OK. This is a new skill they are learning and it will take time before they get used to it. It is useful to let the children know that you cannot fail at mindfulness. They may or may not get frustrated that their mind keeps wandering off. But each time they notice their mind has wandered off, that *is* the meditation. That's the point! It may also be useful to debunk some myths about mindfulness meditation. You are not trying to stop your thoughts, as this is impossible. You are simply becoming more aware of your thoughts, and letting these go when you choose to. As thoughts pop into your mind you notice them, and then watch them drift by like clouds in the sky. The children may come to the wonderful realisation that they are not their thoughts, 'thoughts are not facts' and they don't have to believe them. One final point, the aim of mindfulness is not to become more calm or relaxed. Relaxation may be a pleasant side effect of mindfulness but it is not the goal.

Your attitude as teacher is key, so try to cultivate a light-hearted and kind mindset when meditating with your class. The aim is to give the children a taste of what mindfulness feels like, so we don't want to turn them off it at such a young age. If a practice doesn't go as planned, no big deal. There is always tomorrow. Once, during a lovely listening meditation, a boy in my class accidentally broke wind. He burst out laughing, as did I and the rest of the class. So, we had a laughing meditation instead that day. Try to make meditating with your class an enjoyable experience rather than feeling like a chore.

Here are some tips for meditating with your class:

- **Posture**: Ensure your pupils embody a strong, confident posture, either sitting or standing with a straight spine, shoulders relaxed – like a king or queen on their throne: alert and dignified.

- **Eyes**: Their eyes may be closed or looking down.

- **Hands**: Encourage them to keep their hands still – resting them on their knees or in their lap.

- **Three deep breaths**: They can start by taking three big, deep inhalations that fill their lungs with air – in through the nose, out through the mouth. This begins a virtuous circle of calm in the body.

- **Curiosity and kindness**: It is helpful to cultivate a sense of being curious about what they notice during a practice and also kindness towards themselves if their mind is very busy with thoughts.

- **Singing bowl**: I start and end my meditations by ringing a singing bowl. It is a pleasant way to start and end a practice. I also get the children to take turns to ring the bowl so they feel part of the teaching. You could also use chimes, or prayer bells.

- **Regular practice**: Try to practise every day, at the same time. Mornings work best as it sets you and your class up for the day. Having a routine means you're less likely to forget to do it.

- **Short and sweet**: Keep the meditations short to begin with (one to two minutes) and build from there.

Mindfulness practices

Below, I have suggested five simple mindfulness meditation practices to explore with your class. Your job is to guide your class through the meditations, giving them the instructions. Although you can join in with the practices, you will need to keep your eyes open to ensure that the atmosphere and behaviour is conducive to meditating. There are many practices out there that you can try and I have listed some specialist mindfulness for children books in the 'Further reading and recommended resources' section of this book (p. 182).

It is important to remind the children that, in essence, mindfulness meditation practices are about resting your attention, awareness or focus on one thing at a time. Every time you notice your mind has wandered off (which it will do constantly), you gently bring your attention back to focus on the thing you had intended to focus on. You keep repeating this – focus, mind wandering, back to focusing – for the duration of the practice. This is what strengthens the parts of the brain that control attention and emotional self-regulation.

Breathing buddies

This is a good practice to start with for very young children (three to six years old). I once taught this to my god-daughter when she was feeling quite frantic and she loved it and said it calmed her down.

Choose a cuddly toy to be your 'breathing buddy'. Now, find a space to lie on the floor and place your breathing buddy on your belly. As you breathe in normally, watch as your belly rises and your breathing buddy goes up. As you breathe out, notice your breathing buddy going back down as your belly falls and relaxes. Keep noticing the rise and fall of your breathing buddy as you breathe in and out. If your mind wanders off, that's OK, just return your focus to your breathing buddy going up and down, up and down.

Tummy and chest

This is a practice inspired by the *Paws.b course* created by the charity, Mindfulness in Schools Project (see pp. 33–4). You can perform this practice either sitting on the floor or on a chair, or standing in 'mountain pose' (standing tall, arms and hands relaxed by your side, feet shoulder-width apart).

Start by taking three deep breaths – in through your nose and out through your mouth. Then, as you begin to breathe normally, slowly place one hand on your tummy and one hand on your chest. Feel the breath coming into your body as your chest rises and expands. And then feel the breath leaving your body as it falls away and relaxes. Where do you feel the breath the strongest – in your tummy or in your chest? Are the breaths long or short? Are they deep or shallow? Just notice your breathing with friendly curiosity. See if you can be with the whole of the in-breath and the whole of the out-breath. Be curious about the pause between each in-breath and out-breath. Every time your mind wanders off into thinking mode, simply notice that it has wandered, and gently bring your focus back to your hands resting on your tummy and chest. Let any thoughts drift away like clouds in a bright blue sky. Breathing in...and breathing out.

Walking meditation

If you do this practice indoors, it feels nice to do it without any shoes on. This practice is about walking slowly and deliberately.

Starting in mountain pose with your eyes closed, take your attention down into the soles of your feet. Feel where they connect to the floor, helping you feel grounded and stable. What sensations are in your feet? Is there any tingling or fizzing? Is there any sense of heat or coldness? Be aware of your whole body standing here in mountain pose. When you're ready, open your eyes and focus on your right foot. Slowly peel this foot off the floor. Feel the weight of the foot as you lift it, move it through the air, and then place it slowly down. Notice the weight of your body in this foot as you shift your weight, ready to lift your left foot. Now, slowly peel your left foot off the floor; feel the weight of this foot as you lift it, move it through the air and slowly place it down. As you continue to slowly and deliberately walk, see if you can notice what other parts of the body are involved in helping you walk. Each time your mind drifts off into thinking mode, gently bring your attention back to focusing on the feet. (Allow a few minutes of mindful walking.) And then, come back to standing in mountain pose for a few moments. Gently close your eyes as you become aware of how your body feels, standing here, breathing.

Listening meditation

This listening practice is inspired by an exercise in Eline Snel's book, *Sitting Still Like a Frog* (Snel, 2013). You can do this seated or standing, and it is a lovely practice to do outside when the weather is nice.

Start by taking three deep breaths. As you begin to breathe normally, bring your attention to sounds (leave short pauses between each of the questions to allow the children to notice). What sounds can you hear in this moment? Are the sounds nearby or far away? Are they high- or low-pitched? Are the sounds pleasant or unpleasant? You're not trying to think lots about the sounds, you're just noticing the sounds. Are the sounds outside of yourself? Can you hear any sounds inside yourself? Can you hear yourself breathing? If you're really quiet, can you hear your own heart beating?

Eating meditation

Very often we don't pay close attention to what we eat. Children and adults gobble food down whilst doing something else – either chatting to someone or watching TV. This practice helps children bring a renewed attention to eating. You can do this with any item of food – a raisin works well, or a piece of chocolate (just be sure to check about any food allergies and be mindful about choking risks with younger children). Afterwards, get the children to share what their experience of mindful eating was like. Often a simple raisin has never before tasted so good! Whatever item of food you choose, get your children to start the meditation sitting on a chair by a table.

I would like you to pick up the item of food as if you are seeing it for the very first time. What colours do you notice? Is the texture smooth or bumpy? How does the light reflect off the food? Now, bringing the item up to your nose, take a big, long sniff. What does it smell like? Now, gently run the item across your lips – does it feel soft or hard? Slowly place the item in your mouth but do not chew yet. Move it around your mouth using your tongue. What does it feel like? Are there any flavours around? Notice if your mouth is dry or starting to salivate. When you're ready, slowly begin to bite into it. What sounds can you hear as you bite into it? What can you taste? Is it bitter or sweet or salty? Eventually, swallow your food down and notice any aftertastes in your mouth.

Key points

- Our primitive brains often find it hard to cope with the everyday stresses of modern life and they can get stuck in a stress response cycle. Over time this can exhaust and deplete us, and can lead to anxiety and depression.

- Mindfulness-based interventions have proven very effective in helping people lower levels of stress, anxiety and depression, whilst boosting their immune systems and increasing their levels of resilience and happiness.

- Introducing mindfulness practices into your classroom is fairly simple, but to make it authentic, it helps if you have your own personal mindfulness practice.

- It often works best to meditate with your class at the start of the day, and establishing a regular practice, little and often, is key.

- For younger children, 'Breathing buddies' is a great meditation to start with (see p. 40). It is a fun way to help children learn how to focus on their breathing.

- Experiment with guiding your class through sitting, listening, walking and eating meditations (see pp. 40–2). Keep an open mind and a light heart when you start – meditation is a skill that children will develop the more they practise. Don't lose faith if some meditations don't go to plan and try to have fun with it.

Chapter 3
What went well?

When you arise in the morning, think of what a precious privilege it is to be alive — to breathe, to think, to enjoy, to love.

— Marcus Aurelius

Chapter overview

In this chapter, we'll better understand why brains have a negativity bias and we'll look at powerful ways that we can begin to actually rewire children's brains so that they notice and savour the positives in their lives more.

In theory	In action
• Negativity bias	• What went well?
• Teflon™ for good, Velcro™ for bad	• Thank you letters
• Positive emotions	• Savouring meditation
• Rewiring our brains	• Count your blessings
• Three good things	• Mental time travel
• Gratitude	
• Savouring the past and the future	

In theory

Negativity bias

Have you ever noticed how the news is full of negative stories and how we can't help but be drawn to them? Or how when your headteacher is giving you feedback, you'll forget all of the positive bits and just remember the one negative? According to psychologists, this is because our brains have an innate negativity bias. This is an evolutionary hangover – our ancestors needed to be hyper vigilant on the savannah in order to survive. In short, those hunter-gatherers who spotted the dangers quickly could avoid them (and therefore survive and pass on their genes), but those who stopped to smell a rose or admire a beautiful vista were gobbled up by a lion. So, our brains are primed to look out for bad stuff more than they are tuned to notice the good stuff.

Although it was essential for our hunter-gatherer ancestors to hunt and forage for food, if they didn't find food one day, they could always go searching the next day. However, if they were not paying attention to all of the many threats that were out there too, their hunting days would be over for good. According to neuropsychologist, Rick Hanson, the number one rule in the wild is: 'Eat lunch today – don't *be* lunch today.' (Hanson, 2014, p. 20) Despite the lack of life and death situations for many of us in our modern lives, our brains still react in a very primitive way to threats, as we saw in Chapter 2 (p. 31). Our brains will likely react in a negative way in stressful situations like traffic jams, lesson observations, arguments and even first dates!

The fact is, your brain constantly scans its environment for threats. Even when you're feeling calm and content, without you being aware, your brain is scanning away, looking for negative things. This is why negative stimuli are perceived more quickly than positive stimuli, and why we recognise angry faces more easily than happy ones. Our brains are trying to notice the bad stuff rapidly so we can then take evasive action. And it is our old friend, the amygdala (see Chapter 2, p. 31), who is largely responsible for our negativity bias by triggering the 'fight and flight' response when we sense danger. Every time your amygdala responds to a negative situation, it becomes even more sensitive to negative situations in the future. A vicious circle can arise because, when your amygdala triggers the release of the stress hormone, cortisol, it can weaken and inhibit an area of the brain known as the hippocampus. Hanson points out that this is a problem because, 'The hippocampus puts things in perspective while also calming down your amygdala.' (Hanson, 2014, p. 23) When our brains are caught up in a negativity-bias loop, it can become very hard for us to regain perspective and appreciate the good things that are going on in our lives as well.

Teflon™ for good, Velcro™ for bad

Fear plays a huge part in our brain's negativity bias. Hanson notes that our ancestors could have made two types of mistakes in the past:

1. believing there was a lion hiding in the bushes when there wasn't actually one there, and

2. believing there wasn't a lion in the bush when actually there was.

The first mistake means a bit of needless anxiety, but the cost of the second mistake would have been death. Therefore, our brains have evolved to make the first mistake over and over again to avoid making the second mistake even once. You can see why, when we are fearful, our minds can easily run away with negative thoughts about future events because, in many ways, this is what they are designed to do. There are even parts of the amygdala specifically designed to prevent the unlearning of fear, especially from childhood events (Hanson, 2014, p. 24).

Furthermore, your brain tends to be 'stickier' when it comes to bad experiences. Hanson explains, 'Your brain is like Velcro for negative experiences and Teflon for positive ones.' (Hanson, 2014, p. 27) When you experience something negative, unpleasant, sad or stressful, these implicit memories are hardwired into your brain. We generally learn much faster from pain than pleasure, whereas positive experiences tend to wash over us without leaving much of a trace. We might remember them but they aren't as powerful as our negative memories.

Positive emotions

If our brains are designed to have a negativity bias, then what role do positive emotions play in our lives? Positive emotions are those that feel good or pleasant when we experience them. They range from the feeling of peace we might experience during a walk in the woods, or the feeling of joy when our favourite team wins a match. Psychologist Barbara Fredrickson has done extensive research in this area and believes the top ten positive emotions that people experience the most are:

1. 'love'

2. 'joy'

3. 'gratitude'

4. 'serenity'

5. 'interest'

6. 'hope'

7. 'pride'

8. 'amusement'

9. 'inspiration'

10. 'awe' (Fredrickson, 2013).

Based on her research, Fredrickson developed her 'broaden and build' theory. Whereas negative emotions narrow our focus so we can pay close attention to a specific threat, positive emotions tend to have the opposite effect. When we're in a positive emotional state, we tend to *broaden* our horizons, notice more, and become more creative and flexible in our thinking. We also *build* greater social bonds, which in turn help us to build greater physical and intellectual capabilities. Many studies have shown that people who experience more positive emotions tend to do better in life overall. Professor Paul Dolan explains:

> 'Those who experience better emotions tend to live longer, are in better health, recover from viruses more quickly, take less time off work, are more successful in their careers, are generally more productive, and have happier marriages. In a study of siblings, kids who have a sunnier disposition are more likely to get a degree, get hired and get promoted. Good emotions also…improve our ability to resolve conflicts. Furthermore, those of us who are seen to be in a good mood are thought of as more attractive, which means getting better grades at school and more money at work.' (Dolan, 2015, p. 82)

So, in a nutshell, negative emotions help to keep us alive, but positive emotions improve the *quality* of our lives.

Rewiring our brains

Just because our brains have a negativity bias, this does not mean it has to stay this way. Neuroplasticity is the brain's ability to change, adapt and rewire and we can train our brains to not only notice the positive in our lives more, but actually hardwire these experiences in our brains (Chapter 4 looks at neuroplasticity in more detail, p. 61). Hanson believes that in order for us to do this effectively, we need to stay with positive experiences for longer than normal (for example, maybe ten to 30 seconds). He calls this 'taking in the good.' So, if we are enjoying a nice meal out with family or friends, we have to consciously take in this experience by really noticing what is going on in our minds and our bodies, and savour the experience almost as if it is filling us up from our core. Clearly, becoming more mindful will certainly help with the skill of becoming more aware of those positive present moment experiences. And by taking time to appreciate and savour the good in our lives, we increase the amount of positive emotions we feel. Good feelings experienced today increase the likelihood of experiencing good feelings tomorrow. And each time we stop to appreciate and take in the good in our lives, we grow more neural structure in our brains. Over time, Hanson believes this 'will change your brain, and how you feel and act, in far-reaching ways.' (Hanson, 2009, p. 77)

By regularly looking for chances to take in the good, you can prime the brain to keep on the lookout for positive experiences. These will promote the release of happy hormones, such as dopamine, which in turn make your brain more receptive to positive experiences in the future. This can create a virtuous cycle and even make your brain 'stickier' for positive emotions. Shawn Achor notes that in studies of people who practised taking in the good, 'The better they got at scanning the world for good things…the more good things they saw, without even trying, wherever they looked.' (Achor, 2011, p. 101)

It is important to note that we are not talking about putting a happy, positive spin on everything or ignoring the hard aspects of our lives. This isn't 'positive thinking' – that is, trying to convince ourselves that life is great when the reality is the opposite. Taking in the good is about noticing what is already there. Hanson notes, 'It's about nourishing well-being, contentment, and peace inside that are refuges you can always come from and return to.' (Hanson, 2009, p. 76) There are several exercises you can do to take in the good, which we'll look at now in more detail.

Three good things

A simple, yet powerful, technique used to train our brains to notice the good stuff more is called 'three good things'. This is often an activity attributed to the godfather of positive psychology, Martin Seligman. The research shows that when people write down three things that went well for them each day, it can have a profound effect on their levels of wellbeing. In a famous study carried out by Seligman and his colleagues, participants were asked every evening for one week to write down three things that went well for them, and what caused them. A measure of the participants' wellbeing was taken before they started the activity, immediately after it, and then up to six months later. The results showed that the activity gradually increased people's happiness levels and decreased any of their depressive symptoms over a six-month period. Even though they were only asked to write down their three good things for one week, some of them continued. Those who continued showed the greatest improvement in wellbeing. For those who stopped the exercise, they still remained significantly happier and showed higher levels of optimism (Achor, 2011, p. 101). This shows not only that this exercise is very potent, but also that practising regularly changes your brain the most.

This is a great example of 'taking in the good'. Rather than letting good experiences pass through our minds like water through a sieve, the 'three good things' exercise forces us to recollect a positive experience, write it down and savour it. Every time this exercise is done, it is likely that more neural structure will be built in the area of our brains that process positive emotions, lessening the effect of our negativity bias.

Gratitude

Showing gratitude and appreciation for the good things in our lives has been shown to have very positive effects on our levels of happiness. Gratitude expert, Robert Emmons, has shown that by regularly practising gratitude, people can:

- experience more positive emotions and generally feel happier
- experience fewer negative emotions
- increase their levels of optimism
- boost their immune system
- sleep better
- increase their levels of generosity towards others
- get fitter by exercising more (Emmons, 2010).

Emmons recommends keeping a daily or weekly gratitude diary and writing down things we've appreciated or were grateful for. If you've had a bad day at work and don't feel that anything went particularly well, you can still be grateful that you have a roof over your head, that you have supportive friends or that your children are healthy. Emmons believes the act of writing is important and helps to really internalise the good in our lives.

Another gratitude exercise is known as the 'gratitude letter'. This is where you stop to consider someone in your life who is really important and who you would like to express your gratitude towards. You then write them a letter expressing your thanks and deliver it to them in person. Studies by Seligman and others show that this exercise has significant immediate results in terms of boosting happiness and has positive lasting effects one month later on (King, 2016, p. 263). The power comes from not just reflecting on the positive impact someone has had on your life and consciously expressing your gratitude, but it also comes from the act of sharing it with them. It can be a deeply connecting experience, helping foster positive relationships (which Chapter 1 shows are extremely important for growing happiness, pp. 16–7), and expressing gratitude can also be seen as an act of kindness which also causes a host of positive changes to our happiness levels (see Chapter 7, pp. 113–15).

Savouring the past and the future

Although it is important to savour the present and 'take in the good' as it happens, we certainly shouldn't miss the opportunity to relive those moments again. We can savour the past and derive more happiness from it. One study showed that people who spent 15 minutes a day for three days thinking about happy memories from the past showed increased wellbeing one month later (Smith et al., 2014). Another study showed that when participants were put in a stressful situation, the group that were asked to think of a happy memory for 14 seconds after the event had 15 per cent less cortisol in their bodies than the control group (Speer and Delgado, 2017). Remembering happy memories, it seems, goes right to the heart of the psychological stress response. It can even help to do this exercise with a friend, or in a group, and then share your happy memories afterwards. You can then benefit from 'the doubler effect' (Slatcher and Pennebaker, 2006), which is where you derive as much pleasure from sharing your story as you did from the original experience – effectively doubling its impact.

And let's not miss opportunities to think positively about the future either. When you have a holiday coming up, or a party or special event, have you ever noticed how you can get lots of enjoyment from looking forward to the event? This is known as 'anticipatory enjoyment savouring'. Studies show that positive mental time travel into the future can boost happiness levels and reduce anxiety (Quoidbach et al., 2009).

In action

Children (and teachers!) can be very quick to point out what's going wrong. The following activities flip that tendency around and teach children that there's always something or someone we can appreciate or be grateful for, and that our lives are often full of many small and wonderful things that are actually going well. I have found these practices can be very powerful, especially for more vulnerable children, and they can help foster a culture of gratitude among your tribe.

What went well?

'What went well' is my take on 'three good things'. When I introduced the 'what went well' board in my classroom, it was one of the simplest but most effective things I have done in terms of promoting my class's wellbeing. In practice, it is very easy. Here is how you could do it:

- At the end of the week, give each child a sticky note and ask them to reflect about their week in school. Take a few minutes to remind the class of all the positive experiences they've had and then ask them to write down three things that went well for them. Children have written things like, 'We had a fun PE lesson playing dodgeball!', 'I had a good playtime playing with my friends', 'I enjoyed making models of teeth in science'.

- Each child gets to choose one of their 'what went wells' to share with the class (so benefitting from 'the doubler effect') before handing you their sticky note to put up on your 'what went well' display (see example in Figure 3.1).

- You can download a free 'what went well' display banner using the following link: **www.teachappy.co.uk/resources-and-downloads**.

Figure 3.1: A 'what went well' display

- Give your positive week a cheer and a round of applause and then it is home time!

- You could also create a big 'what went well' book (see Figure 3.2), in which all the sticky notes are saved each week. Store the book in your book corner. Children in my class often choose to read it to remind themselves of the previous good times we've had as a class.

This idea can work beautifully at home too. One parent told me that her son had told her about 'what went well' and that her family had started to share one good thing from their day before they ate dinner. It had such a positive effect that she introduced it into her workplace – before any meeting that she chaired, she would ask her team what had gone well for them that day. It changed the tone of her meetings for the better!

Figure 3.2: Team Picasso's 'what went well' book

I love doing 'what went well' for many reasons. Firstly, it is great to hear the small things that my class have enjoyed or are grateful for. Secondly, it is such a lovely sharing experience in which your class members get to share and listen to each other's positive experiences (which often include the other class members). Thirdly, I know that bit by bit I'm helping rewire my own, and my children's brains to spot the positive more and savour those experiences. Fred, aged nine, summed it up nicely when he said, 'I like "what went well" because even if I have a bad Friday, it makes me reflect on the week and find something good, so I always leave school for the weekend feeling positive.'

Tales from the classroom

Peter joined my class part way through a year. He was a shy boy who had experienced a tough start to life. Growing up in a house where he witnessed domestic violence, he was taken into care and separated from his siblings. Eventually, he was adopted at eight years old and that was when I met him. Needless to say, Peter did not enjoy doing the 'what went well' exercise when it came to it. 'Nothing good has happened,' he would say every Friday afternoon. Either I or my teaching assistant would sit

---

down with Peter and help him write down his three good things. We would have to remind him of the good pieces of work he'd completed that week, or maybe the goal he scored at football practice. Reluctantly, Peter would write them down and choose one to share with the class. Each week was the same – a resistance to acknowledge the good stuff. But, over time, the resistance became less as Peter got better at thinking of his own good things. Bit by bit, we'd make small, positive steps forward until one week something rather special happened. It was a frantic Friday afternoon. It was right at the end of the day and I was trying to give out letters, remind children of their home-learning task, as well as answering the class phone so the office could tell me which child was going home with which adult! With about five minutes to go before I sent the children home, I felt a tap on my leg. I looked down and saw Peter staring back at me. 'You forgot to do our what went wells, Mr Bethune,' said Peter grinning up at me. 'Yes, I have!' I replied, beaming back at him. My class were quite late going home that day. And it was Peter's fault. He wanted us to share our good things before we left school.

Thank you letters

The thank you letter exercise is an effective way to help children practise gratitude more regularly. Why not try this with your class at various points in the year?

- Show your class a short video on gratitude from the BBC *Happiness Challenge* series (a short collection of videos that investigate if carrying out certain activities could make you happier). You can find the video on YouTube here: **www.youtube.com/watch?v=JsIPXwr9BQE**. It shows two people sharing their gratitude letters with important people in their lives and it is quite moving (I never fail to well up when watching it!). Not only does the video provide a good opportunity to discuss why doing nice things for others can make people cry, but it also explains why writing gratitude letters can boost your happiness levels.

- Give your class a moment to think of someone in their lives who does a lot for them and to whom they'd like to show gratitude. Then ask them to write a letter thanking that person for everything they have done. It helps if they give specific things they are thankful for (e.g. helping them with their homework, being cooked delicious dinners, listening to their worries, etc.). The children's task then is simply to give their letter to their special person.

- As an alternative, children can write a gratitude postcard, which you can download using this link: **www.teachappy.co.uk/resources-and-downloads**.

This is a really lovely activity to get children to do. Some children choose to write letters to their friends in the class, some write them to parents or grandparents, some even choose to write them for their teachers (I have kept every gratitude letter I've ever received). The children benefit from the act of reflecting and appreciating all of the people who are important to them, plus they get to experience how powerful it can be to let someone know that they are appreciated. This teaches children the art of cherishing and investing in their positive relationships.

Savouring meditation

I have guided my classes through savouring meditations at various points in the year. They are nice exercises to do to show the children that they have the ability to recall happy memories whenever they need to. Happy memories can be like an inner refuge that we can retreat to when we need to give ourselves a boost.

Try the following guided savouring meditation with your children, and afterwards see who would like to share their happy memories:

Sitting like a king or queen on your throne, ensure your spine is straight but your shoulders are relaxed. Start by taking three deep breaths into your belly. Breathe out slowly. As you begin to breathe normally, bring to mind a happy memory from your past. It can be any memory where you feel safe and happy. Maybe it's a meal, a party or a celebration. What can you see as you look around? Are you by yourself or are other people there? If you're with others, notice what their facial expressions are like – are they laughing and smiling? What sounds can you hear? Is there music playing, or people talking? Are there any strong smells about – the aroma of food, the smell of nature, or people's aftershave or perfume? Don't be afraid to smile as you relive this happy time from your life. Notice how you feel in your body – are there any strong sensations present? Really turn the volume and brightness up on your happy memory, making it louder and brighter in your mind. Stay with this memory and imagine it filling up your whole body as if it were an empty vase. Every time your mind wanders off, just bring your attention back to your happy memory and all of the feelings that come with it.

- Ask the children if anyone would like to share their happy memories. Notice if any themes come up, such as the fact that a lot of our happiest times involve other people and discuss why this might be with your class (most of the happiness research shows that close personal relationships are one of the biggest factors that contribute to our happiness).

- As an extension, see if your class can identify which of the top ten positive emotions they experienced during the meditation (pp. 47–8).

- Be aware that this exercise can sometimes bring up a mixture of emotions. Some happy memories can involve feelings of sadness too, particularly if they involve people who are no longer in the child's life. With sensitivity and care, these moments can provide opportunities to explore the close relationship between happiness and sadness.

Count your blessings

An effective way to shift your pupils' attention away from what they don't have and on to what they do have, is to get them to do the following 'count your blessings' exercise:

- Give the children a sheet of paper and ask them to make a list of all of the things in their life that they are grateful for or lucky to have, that maybe other children around the world lack. You could do this as a timed activity and see how many things they can write down in two minutes.

- Ask the children to share their lists with a partner.

- As a whole class, ask if anything surprising appeared on the list. For example, children might be surprised that they could show gratitude for having comfy slippers! Draw out that we can be grateful for the smallest thing that makes our lives that little bit more comfortable, safe and enjoyable.

Mental time travel

We don't just have to savour the past. We can savour and positively anticipate the future. This next practice has been inspired by Vanessa King's fantastic book, *10 Keys to Happier Living* (which in turn was inspired by research led by Jordi Quoidbach at the University of Liège). Why not have a go with your class and see what impact it has?

- Spend five minutes at the end of the day trying to imagine three positive events that could reasonably happen tomorrow. They can be small things like anticipating a fun maths lesson or a good playtime playing with friends, or watching TV on the sofa snuggled up to family.

- Once they have thought of three things, get them to jot them down on a piece of paper.

- Try this experiment for one or two weeks and after the time period is up, ask the children: 'Did it make you feel any happier?'

Not only does this activity help the children's day end on a positive note (remember 'peak-ending' from Chapter 1 (pp. 20–1) shows us that if our days end well, we will largely rate the whole day as positive), but also it is good to help them positively anticipate small things that could happen the next day at school or at home.

Key points

- Our brains have developed a negativity bias that looks for bad stuff and stores it quickly in our memories so we can try to avoid those situations in the future. This has aided our survival but sometimes undermines our happiness.

- Conversely, positive emotions enhance our quality of life. They help us be more creative, and lead to a host of benefits such as increased levels of happiness, better health, stronger relationships and longer lives.

- We can retrain our brains to notice the positive more by taking in the good. By regularly noticing and savouring what is going well in our lives, we create more neural structure in the positive regions of our brains.

- Every week get your children to do the 'what went well' exercise. Get them to reflect on three things that went well for them, and share one of these with the rest of the class.

- Throughout the year, encourage your class to write thank you letters to important people in their lives. Expressing gratitude boosts your levels of wellbeing and physical health too.

- Guide your class through a savouring meditation so that positive experiences from the past can be relived, so they get to experience the happy hormones again in the present.

- Get your children to do a 'count your blessings' two-minute exercise. How many things can they show appreciation for in such a short space of time?

- Time travel with your class into the future by spending some time thinking about three positive things that could happen the next day. Do this for a week to see if worries decrease and happiness increases.

Chapter 4
Neuroplasticity – your elastic plastic brain

The brain is wider than the sky.

– Emily Dickinson

Chapter overview

Our brains are arguably the most powerful and important organ in our body. Yet relatively little is known about the brain and how it functions compared to other parts of the body. In this chapter, we'll take a peek inside our heads to see what the latest findings in neuroscience can reveal about this mysterious orb, so we can teach children more about how it works, how it contributes to their happiness and how they can best look after it.

In theory	In action
• The elastic plastic brain	• Mini neuroscientists
• Old-fashioned computer brain	• Brain goals
• Neural Darwinism	• Plastic(ine) brain
• Some basic brain facts	• Brain health
• Happy hormones	• Happy hormones
• Brain health	

In theory

The elastic plastic brain

It used to be thought that after childhood people's brains were fixed in terms of their form and what they could do. This idea has been proved to be completely wrong. Neuroscientists are now certain that all brains, young and old, are plastic. By that they mean that our brains can be shaped, influenced and moulded by our thoughts, actions and experiences. Not just once but over and over again. Old dogs certainly can be taught new tricks (it might just take them a few more attempts to master them than their puppy counterparts). Neuroplasticity is the term used to describe this and it means that our brains have the ability to change their structure and function in significant ways.

It's possible to peer inside our brains using MRI scanners and this technology has shown, for example, that virtuoso violinists have larger areas of the brain that control the fingers and have way more neural activity in these parts of the brain. Similarly, London taxi drivers who complete 'the knowledge' (memorising 60,000 streets in London and over 100,000 places of note) show a significant growth in their hippocampus – an area of the brain associated with creating spatial memory (Maguire et al., 2000). Once these taxi drivers retire, their hippocampus shrinks back to 'normal' size again. Interestingly, people who are born deaf perceive objects in their peripheral vision in their visual cortex (the part of the brain that helps with sight) but also in their auditory cortex – the part of the brain that would normally process sound. Richard Davidson explains: 'It is as if the auditory cortex, tired of enforced inactivity as a result of receiving no signals from the ears, took upon itself a regimen of job retraining, so that it now processes visual signals.' (Davidson and Begley, 2012, p. 167) Indeed, studies even show that as we become happier, the left region of the pre-frontal cortex becomes more active and can grow in size (Davidson, 2004). Our brains are amazingly fluid and versatile. They are in a constant state of flux and can literally change shape.

Old-fashioned computer brain

Scientists used to believe the idea that our brain is like a computer, but this is now an outdated concept. Dr John Ratey says that the brain is 'more like an ecosystem than a machine.' (Ratey, 2003, p. 11) Unlike a computer with its predictable outcomes depending on what you program into it, the brain is so complex and malleable that, according to Ratey, 'It is virtually impossible to predict how a given factor will influence its state.' (Ratey, 2003, p. 11) The computer–brain analogy also implies that brains are devoid of emotions and that they plan, remember and process in very mechanical ways, but this simply is not true. In fact, in his book, *The Emotional Life of Your Brain*, Davidson argues that all brain processes pass through the parts of the brain that handle your emotions *before* they then are dealt with by the more 'logical' parts of your brain (Davidson and Begley, 2012). In essence, all logical thought has been influenced by your emotions first. Davidson shares Ratey's view that brains can be unpredictable and he strongly argues against a 'one-size-fits-all' approach when trying to understand how people respond to different life events. Davidson and Begley state, 'I've seen thousands of people who share similar backgrounds respond in dramatically different ways to the same life event.' (Davidson and Begley, 2012, p. 2)

Any teacher or parent will know that children's brains work in mysterious ways! You teach the same lesson to a class of 30 children and you sometimes get 30 different responses and interpretations. Psychologist Alison Gopnik argues that there's a very good evolutionary reason for why children behave and learn in often very unique ways. By producing a 'wide, variable and unpredictable mix of children', each with a distinct brain, temperament, set of skills, strengths and weaknesses, Gopnik believes that it has allowed the human species to adapt to an unpredictable and changing culture and environment (Gopnik, 2016, p. 27). Our breadth in variety has allowed humans to flourish on Earth because, within a tribe, there will be someone whose unique personality and traits will suit any given situation. This is a useful reminder to teachers. Children's brains are not computers to be uploaded with data. Children behave, think and learn in unique and varied ways because that is what they are meant to do.

Neural Darwinism

There is a theory developed by Nobel laureate and neurologist Gerald Edelman about the brain that is similar to Darwin's theory of 'natural selection' and it's called 'neural Darwinism'. The theory explains why neuroplasticity even exists – that is, why our brains are able to change to suit our environment and experiences, and why our brains can learn something and then unlearn it. Edelman explains that some neurons form connections that stay intact and become strong, whereas others do not and die off in a process that resembles natural selection. It's as if neurons form connections and compete with other neurons for survival. The strongest and most adaptable neurons and connections survive in a battle of survival of the fittest. This theory gave rise to the saying, 'Neurons that fire together, wire together.' This means that the more we rehearse certain actions and thoughts (from practising penalty kicks, to learning our lines in the school play), the more those neurons will fire and form connections that can become hardwired in the brain. On the other hand, the phrase 'Use it or lose it' explains how if you don't keep exercising those neurons and connections, they can slowly weaken and could be lost. In this way, our brains work just like a muscle. The more we work out in the gym, the bigger and stronger our muscles get. The moment we stop exercising we begin to lose that muscle mass and our fitness levels decline. And so it is with our brains. The more we exercise them, the more neural connections we make and certain parts of the brain grow. But once we stop practising or exercising them, those brain regions begin to shrink back to their previous sizes.

Some basic brain facts

Our brains are fascinating organs and neuroscientists are discovering more and more about them all the time. Below are some of the brain facts they have discovered:

- The adult brain is about 1.5kg of tissue containing on average 100 billion neurons.
- A neuron is a cell in the brain that sends and receives signals to and from other neurons.
- Each neuron has one axon (axons are the main way by which neurons pass information on and *teach* other neurons) and up to 100,000 dendrites (which are the main ways by which neurons get information and *learn* from other neurons).
- The theoretical number of different connections possible in a single brain is 40 quadrillion (or 40,000,000,000,000,000).

- It is believed that most learning and development in the brain is through the process of strengthening and weakening these connections.

- A neuron receives signals from other neurons usually as a burst of electro-chemicals called neurotransmitters. These signals tell a neuron to fire or not. In turn, this neuron will send signals to other neurons telling them to fire or not.

- Our brains actually produce small amounts of electricity when these signals are sent. Some believe they produce enough to power a dim light bulb!

- Even though your brain makes up only two per cent of the body's weight, it uses up to 25 per cent of the body's oxygen and glucose.

- Your brain never really switches off – it uses about the same amount of energy when you're asleep, as when you're trying to work out how to explain neuroscience to a seven-year old!

Happy hormones

There are many chemicals the human body releases that contribute to human happiness and wellbeing. They fall under various neuroscientific labels such as neurotransmitters, neuromodulators and neuropeptides. For simplicity, I will refer to them as 'happy hormones'. Below is a very brief summary of some of the key happy hormones that affect our wellbeing:

- **Serotonin**: This regulates our mood, sleep and digestion. When people suffer from depression, any antidepressants they are given aim to boost its effects. Our diet can affect our levels of serotonin as can our exposure to natural light. Eating well and getting outdoors are two ways to help regulate our serotonin levels.

- **Dopamine**: Often called the 'learning neurotransmitter' (Ratey, 2003, p. 122), it helps us pay attention, and is involved in our 'reward system' – that is, when something good happens to us, we get a rush of dopamine that makes us feel good. It gets released when we achieve something and, also, when we laugh and find something funny.

- **Endorphins**: They help protect us against stress, reduce our experience of pain and produce pleasure. They are often released during exercise, hence the 'high' runners feel after a run.

- **Oxytocin**: This promotes prosocial behaviour and bonding between people. It helps us to be kind and show empathy towards others. It often gets released when you hug or hold hands with someone you like, or even when you stroke a pet. It can also get released when you are kind to others.

There are other happy hormones, such as **noradrenaline** and **endocannabinoids**, but for the sake of teaching children, I stick to the above four.

All of the happy hormones listed above are types of neurotransmitters, meaning they help our neurons communicate with each other and, therefore, they help us to learn better. They also positively impact on our health, lowering stress levels and boosting our immune system. Feeling good, does us good.

Brain health

As with other major organs in our bodies, for the brain to work optimally, it is essential to take care of it. According to Ratey, 'Almost anything we do, eat, or drink can affect the brain,' (Ratey, 2003, p. 6), which means we need to be careful about what we do, eat and drink in order to affect the brain positively. Let's take a look at a few ways to keep your brain in tip-top condition.

Water

It is believed that around 75 per cent of the brain is made up of water. This means that drinking healthy levels of water is important to maintaining your brain function. Studies have shown that dehydration can impair short- and long-term memory and affect our ability to focus and concentrate. If you do not drink enough water your neurons start to become less efficient (Gowin, 2010). Dr John Briffa claims that, 'Dehydration is quite simply one of the biggest, under-recognised drains on performance.' (Briffa, 2014, p. 102) How much water is enough? Well, many factors will affect the amount you need (such as age, gender, the weather, physical activity, etc.) but generally children need to aim for six to eight cups of fluid a day in addition to the water they'll naturally get from foods (British Nutrition Foundation, 2016). One of the best indicators of how hydrated you are is the colour of your urine (thirst is often a later sign we might be dehydrated) (Briffa, 2014, p. 104). If your urine is straw-coloured or pale yellow that is a good sign you are well hydrated. Dark yellow urine is a sure sign you need to get straight to the tap!

Diet

'A balanced diet is the best brain medicine' (Ratey, 2003, p. 370). We should be aiming to eat well every day and take in a wide variety of nutrients. Hanson believes that: 'More than anything, this means eating lots of protein and vegetables.' (Hanson, 2009, p. 228) Carbohydrates are important too though, as they increase the amount of an amino acid in the brain called tryptophan, which is the building block for the neuro-transmitter serotonin. Serotonin is possibly the most important chemical in your body for maintaining a good mood. Sugar intake should be minimised wherever possible. Although the brain uses a large amount of the body's glucose to function, ingesting sugar can cause glucose spikes, followed by a sugar crash where glucose levels fall dramatically, leaving your brain feeling sluggish and tired. In fact, too much sugar can actually be toxic for the brain. As with most things in life, balance is the key.

Sleep

A good night's sleep is not only good for maintaining brain health, but it can help regulate your emotions and even help you learn better. When people experience REM sleep (rapid eye movement sleep is where active dreaming takes place), it is thought that memories get moved from their short-term memory (what you learned and experienced that day – also known as your 'working memory') into their long-term memory (so you can retrieve that information tomorrow and into the future). When you are dreaming, it is as if your brain is rehearsing what it has learned that day, and this rehearsing strengthens the neurons involved in that activity. However, poor sleep negatively affects people's concentration, coordination, memory and mood. As mindfulness expert Jon Kabat-Zinn explains, 'When we are sleep deprived, our thinking, our moods, and our behaviour can become erratic and unreliable, our body becomes exhausted and we become more susceptible to getting sick.' (Kabat-Zinn, 2013, p. 363) Many experts believe one of the biggest barriers to children getting a good night's sleep is the use of electronic devices near bedtime. These devices emit blue light, which tricks the brain into thinking it is daytime and, therefore, preventing the release of the sleep-inducing hormone, melatonin. Perhaps a book in bed would be a better choice than a tablet.

Exercise

Movement is good for the brain. When we exercise, our heart pumps more blood and oxygen to the brain. Our brains thrive on blood and oxygen, as they need it to think, function and learn. Exercise boosts our mood and releases happy hormones like endorphins and dopamine. We'll look at the effects of exercise on our brains and bodies in a lot more detail in Chapter 9 (p. 143) but, for now, get moving to keep those neurons firing and wiring!

In action

Without question, when I started teaching my classes about the brain, those lessons were easily some of the most engaging lessons I have taught. That's partly due to my natural interest and passion for learning about neuroscience, but it's also because I believe most young children are budding neuroscientists. As soon as you start to teach young children about the brain, they will ask so many thoughtful questions, which you simply won't have the answers for! Children love discovering more about the brain because, ultimately, it allows them to better understand themselves and the people around them. In my opinion, this is one of the highest forms of learning and helps develop their emotional intelligence.

Mini neuroscientists

Teaching mini neuroscience lessons to your children may sound daunting (especially if you don't know much about neuroscience), but the basics explained above are really all the children need to know for now and there are some excellent resources online to help you out. A great place to start is the BBC Brainsmart videos (although the BBC has archived this resource now, the videos are still available online). Here's how you can help your pupils become mini neuroscientists:

- Show the video, *Meet Your Brain* (**www.bbc.co.uk/programmes/ p005m333**) to your class, as it neatly sums up that our brains are capable of amazing things and, through effort and practice, our brains form new connections and learn new things. This also introduces the children to the idea of 'neuroplasticity', and teaches them that, like a muscle, we can grow our brains. This is a great way to pique the children's interest and the visuals show what neurons look like and how they form connections.

- You could follow up with a session on stress by showing the Brainsmart video called *Managing Stress* (**www.bbc.co.uk/ programmes/p00hylmg**). You could discuss with your class what stress is, why we need it in small amounts (like in the stretch zone to help us focus and learn – see Chapter 5, p. 77), but how too much is not good for our health or the brain. Talk about the strategies for managing stress from the video but then ask the children if they have any other stress-busting techniques.

- Invest in some books about the brain for your book corner and allow the children to do their own research. They could share with the class any interesting facts they discover. It was a pupil that taught me that babies' brains have more neurons than adults' brains! See 'Further reading and recommended resources' for some recommended books about the brain for children (pp. 181–8).

Brain goals

Once you have taught your first neuroscience lesson, and shown the *Meet Your Brain* video, you could try the following brain goals exercise:

- Ask your children to think of the things they are good at. It might be things in school like writing stories, knowing their times tables or reading, or maybe it's things outside of school like doing tricks on their BMX or singing their favourite pop songs. Then ask two questions:

1. Were you always good at those things?

2. How did you get good at those things?

The children invariably conclude that it was through practising and putting in effort, that they improved at those things.

- Next, ask them to think about three things that they either can't do now, or aren't very good at, but that they wish to improve at with effort and practice. Maybe suggest that two of the things be school-related and one can be something outside of school. It helps if they are fairly specific because then it is easier to tell if you have achieved that goal at a later stage (e.g. 'I want to learn how to do neat joined-up handwriting' is more specific than 'I want to get better at English').

- Then give each child an outline of a brain and ask them to write down their three brain goals and colour in the brains to make them eye-catching. These brains can go up on a 'brain power' display you

Figure 4.1: A 'Brain power' display with brain goals attached

could make for your classroom (see Figure 4.1) or your 'stretch zone' display (see Chapter 5 for more on this, p. 77).

- You can download a 'brain power' display banner using this link: **www.teachappy.co.uk/resources-and-downloads**.

- At the end of the term, take the brains down and reflect on the goals to see whether the children have achieved them. Has our handwriting improved? Do we know our eight times table? Can we do a wheelie on our BMX? You can celebrate the things they have achieved and tick them off (our brains normally release dopamine when we tick things off our to-do lists or achieve our goals), and they can think about what they need to do next if there are some goals yet to achieve.

This is a simple yet effective goal-setting exercise that can be done at the start and end of each term. Unlike the, often arbitrary, targets teachers set for their pupils, these goals are more meaningful to the children because they have chosen them. This activity reinforces to the children that their learning is their responsibility and that to achieve anything requires effort, persistence and practice.

Plastic(ine) brain

One of the key messages you want to get across to the children is just how malleable our brains are. When children begin to understand that their brains (and intelligence) are not fixed, and that they have the power to shape them through focus, effort and practice, they really start to develop more of a growth mindset (more about that in the next chapter!). In any lesson that I teach, I will usually refer to the brain and how the children's neurons will be connecting up each time they learn something new or repeat a new skill.

I try to bring the brain into all areas of the curriculum. For instance, in art, when working with clay, we decided to make models of our brains. We had learned that our brains have two halves (hemispheres), connected by a thick band of nerve fibres (the corpus callosum). Amazingly, we discovered that our left side of the brain controls movement on our right side of the body, and the right side of the brain controls movement on the left side of our body. So, using the clay, we made these two hemispheres and made them the size of our two clenched fists put together (which is roughly the size of your brain). It was a fun way to learn more about the brain and to get the children to think more about this amazing tool they have within their skulls! It also reinforced the idea that our brains are plastic and malleable because we literally moulded our brains out of clay. If clay sounds too messy, then you could use Plasticine™ or sticky tack.

Tales from the classroom

One class I taught, Team Picasso, were so enthusiastic about the brain, we decided to do our class assembly on it (we sacked off the Romans, which was our topic that term, and focused on the brain instead). We used our computing lesson time to use the laptops and tablets to carry out our research. I organised the children into groups and then gave each group a topic to research – happy hormones, amazing brain facts, mindfulness and the brain, sleep, exercise and diet. With their research and ideas, we co-wrote a script, dressed up as neuroscientists in our white lab coats (our mums' and dads' white shirts – see Figure 4.2), and delivered an amazing assembly called 'Brain Power'. The assembly was a real hit and now every teacher in the school teaches mini neuroscience lessons to their classes at various points in the year.

Brain health

It is all very well teaching children about their amazing brains but, unless they are looking after them, they may not actually be able to remember all of this cool new neuroscience stuff! Therefore, an essential part of teaching children about their brains is teaching them how to look after them. Try these ideas to encourage your pupils to take good care of their brains:

- Show your class the BBC Brainsmart video, *Look After Your Brain* (**www.bbc.co.uk/programmes/p0074vst**). It covers the areas of diet, water and exercise, which you can then look at in more detail.

Figure 4.2: Team Picasso dressed up as neuroscientists for their class assembly on the brain

Diet

This is such an important part of maintaining brain health and optimising functionality.

- A great online resource that teaches children about what a balanced diet looks like is **www.foodafactoflife.org.uk**. It reinforces three key facts: food is a basic requirement of life; people choose different types of food; and we need a variety and balance of food to stay healthy. There is a fun, interactive game the children can play online where they sort foods into different food groups, and there is a teacher's guide with lesson plans and ideas if you want to do a whole unit of work around food (see 'Further reading and recommended resources', p. 186).

- Another good idea is to share a healthy breakfast in your class. Maybe once a half-term, either ask parents to donate fruit, cereals (healthy ones that are low in sugar!), breads and spreads, or see if the school budget will stretch, and have a class breakfast. It is such a nice way to start the day and helps foster that sense of tribe and family in your classroom, whilst letting the children experience different types of food.

- You could also set up a cookery club at your school – get children preparing food, trying new foods out and learning about food hygiene.

Water

I fully understand how frustrating it can be when you want to start a lesson and several children want to get up to have a drink (especially if they've just come in from playtime when they had access to several water fountains!) but without that water their brains may not be in the best condition to learn what you're about to teach them anyway. Rather than being specific about how much water your children should be drinking, allow them to self-regulate, but teach them to check the colour of their pee! Every time they have a loo break, if their pee is pale yellow they're all good. If it's darker yellow, have a drink. Get into the habit of encouraging regular drink breaks at the start of and during lessons. If your children have water bottles in school, allow them on their tables. Little and often is best but keep those brains hydrated!

Exercise

To maximise your children's ability to think and learn, and be healthy and happy, we need to give them opportunities to exercise every day. Get them moving during lessons by trying the following:

- Have little breaks and do star jumps.
- Stop a lesson and get your class to do a lap of the playground before carrying on.
- Introduce the 'Daily mile' to get your children running every day (see Chapter 9, p. 150).
- Set up some lessons during the day in which the children need to get out of their seats and move around the class to either get information from other tables, or so they can progress to the next part of the lesson.

Don't just wait for your weekly PE lesson to get the children moving – it needs to be a daily activity. Chapter 9 has a lot more ideas on how to incorporate exercise seamlessly into your daily routine (pp. 149–57).

Happy hormones

In the classes that I teach, the children know what happy hormones are and some of the ways that cause them to be released in our bodies. I think this is important because it teaches them that they can directly affect how they are feeling by taking some action. Feeling a little glum? Try going for a walk or a run outside to release serotonin and endorphins. A bit stressed? Try a mindfulness practice or ask a friend for a hug to release oxytocin. This is another means by which you can get children to acknowledge and recognise how they are feeling and decide whether they need to take any action. This complements the mindfulness practices very well. It means that children are not powerless in the face of difficult feelings or moods.

- Why not create four posters in your class, one for each of the main happy hormones (see pp. 65–6), explaining how the hormone affects your happiness and what activities help that hormone to be released?

- Refer to the posters when you think that hormone might have been released. For example, after some exercise with your class, you might refer to the endorphins poster and say, 'We know exercise releases endorphins into our bodies, so enjoy that feeling of your stress levels reducing, and any feelings of pleasure.'

The point is to get the children thinking about how their behaviour and actions can positively affect how they feel.

Key points
- Our brains are amazingly plastic, meaning that they can adapt and change. All of us, young and old, can learn new things and master new tricks with practice and effort.
- We learn when our neurons grow stronger connections with each other.
- Happy hormones are released by the body, which can help boost our mood, reduce stress, protect the immune system and make us feel good. These hormones (also called neurotransmitters) help our brains to learn better and grow.

- We must look after our brains by staying hydrated, eating a healthy and balanced diet and exercising regularly.
- Children show a natural fascination about learning about the brain and this enthusiasm helps turn them into budding neuroscientists.
- Teach children more about their brains. Reinforce the key message that their brains are not fixed and they can strengthen and grow them just like a muscle.
- Help children look after their brains by having regular water breaks in class, sharing breakfasts and healthy food at school, and getting your children off their seats and moving more.

Chapter 5
The stretch zone

Do one thing every day that scares you.

— Eleanor Roosevelt

Chapter overview

In this chapter, we'll look at what it takes to help children leave the safety of their comfort zones so they can fulfil their potential. We'll understand why their brains learn better in the 'stretch zone' and how it contributes to fostering a 'growth mindset'. We'll even look at the paradox of how experiencing some stress and discomfort can actually contribute to children's overall sense of wellbeing.

In theory	In action
• The stretch zone	• Stretch zone display
• Struggle	• Beautiful mistakes
• Growth mindset	• 'Flearning'
• Praise	• Be like the penguin
• The mouse in the maze	• Youcubed.org

In theory

The stretch zone

Harvard psychologist Tal Ben-Shahar developed the concept of 'the stretch zone'. He believes that by getting people to step outside of their comfort zones and into their stretch zone, they can function optimally and achieve to their fullest potential. Figure 5.1 illustrates the three zones of learning and growth. In the centre is the comfort zone.

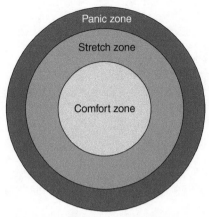

Figure 5.1: The different zones of growth and learning

When we operate in our comfort zone, the work is not challenging us. This means that our brains are not being stimulated that much, neural activity will be low and we don't really learn anything new here. Our comfort zone is not a bad place to be (in fact, it can be very restorative and good for our wellbeing to spend time here) but, in terms of learning, it can be a bit of a cul-de-sac. You get to the end of the road and there's not much there.

In the stretch zone, however, our brains really come alive. To continue with my road analogy, the stretch zone is like being on a wide, open road with little traffic – it can take you to places you've never been before, you'll see some amazing sights and the journey can be really exciting. Your neurons will be firing and wiring, happy hormones will be flooding your system and learning becomes intrinsically rewarding and motivating.

The 'panic zone' though is like being on a Formula One race track, on a bicycle, with no helmet. Quite frankly, it's just plain scary. Your brain shuts down as you enter into 'fight or flight' mode. You don't learn anything new here, apart from to avoid this scenario in the future at all costs.

The job of the teacher, therefore, is to help their pupils spend more time in the stretch zone, by coaxing them out of their comfort zones and supporting them when they stray into the panic zone.

Stress and the stretch zone

The stretch zone by its very nature involves children leaving a place where they feel comfortable and doing work, performing tasks and operating in a place where they will feel discomfort and a certain level of stress. Now this may seem counter-intuitive when trying to boost the levels of wellbeing in your pupils. However, Louis Cozolino agrees that teaching children to handle a certain level of stress is good for their development and is where their brains really begin to flourish. Cozolino notes, 'Keeping students in a neuroplastic "sweet spot" of arousal is a core element in the art of teaching.' (Cozolino, 2014, pp. 81–2)

Figure 5.2 below illustrates where this 'sweet spot' occurs. Two psychologists, Robert Yerkes and John Dodson (1908) published a famous paper on the relationship between learning and stress, and their findings became known as the 'inverted-U curve'. Their research showed that, for people to learn at optimal levels, the level of challenge, stress or arousal needs to be not too low or too high. If the challenge is too easy, children get bored and switch off (comfort zone) but if the challenge is too hard, children can enter the 'panic zone' and the level of stress inhibits any learning. It turns out that moderate levels of stress (characteristic of the

Classic inverted-U curve

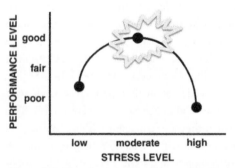

Figure 5.2: The classic inverted-U curve graph showing where the 'sweet spot' of performance occurs. Reproduced with kind permission from Professor Daniela Kaufer from her presentation 'What can neuroscience research teach us about teaching?' (Kaufer, 2011)

type people experience in the stretch zone) lead to maximum levels of learning and performance.

When Yerkes and Dodson carried out their research in the early 20th century, the ability to scan people's brains didn't exist but modern neuroscience now backs up their findings. It turns out that at moderate levels of stress and arousal, our amygdala releases small amounts of hormones (such as cortisol and norepinephrine) that are crucial to learning. These hormones stimulate the hippocampus (which is a core part of the brain involved in forming memories) and neural plasticity is maximised (McGaugh, 2004; McGaugh et al., 1993). However, when we become too anxious about the task at hand, the amygdala floods our system with these same hormones that then inhibit the hippocampus and stop new learning from occurring. If children are too stressed or anxious, they simply cannot learn.

Teachers really need to carefully manage stress levels in the classroom. By allowing just the right amount of stress, you take your class on a journey into the stretch zone and there anything becomes possible.

Struggle

When we are in the stretch zone, the task, whatever it may be, will be challenging to us and we will inevitably struggle at times, but when we struggle there is a real opportunity for deep learning to occur. By making tasks harder for children, by introducing what some psychologists call 'desirable difficulties' (Bjork and Bjork, 2011), we actually increase the chances of this learning hardwiring into their long-term memory. Ben-Shahar also warns parents and teachers against protecting children too much from struggle. He notes, 'Educators, especially parents, confuse struggle with pain; wanting to protect their children from pain, they cater to their children's every wish and rescue them from every challenge.' (Ben-Shahar, 2008, p. 88) Therefore, teachers need to allow their pupils to struggle with tasks in the classroom and, at times, with life in the school community. This means not rescuing pupils when they are struggling with a problem in a lesson, or trying to solve a falling-out with a friend in the playground. Of course, you can be there to offer support and some guidance but it is about allowing your pupils to struggle and find their own way through.

Again, this may seem contradictory when we are trying to foster our children's levels of happiness. Why wouldn't we rescue our children when we can see they are struggling? But to rescue them denies them a crucial aspect of learning. Only when we allow our children to struggle with a problem will they experience the deep satisfaction that comes from overcoming challenges. Ben-Shahar goes on to say, 'Struggles and hardships and challenges are a necessary component of an emotionally rich life; there are no easy shortcuts to happiness.' (Ben-Shahar, 2008, p. 89) So the stretch zone involves struggle. In fact, it actively seeks out struggle. It is designed to stretch your pupils beyond what they can currently do and in doing this, their brains are turned on for learning and they get to experience the joy of overcoming an obstacle and rising up to a challenge.

Growth mindset

The stretch zone supports and complements psychologist Carol Dweck's theories on mindset. Dweck's research shows that in certain areas of our lives we may either have a 'fixed mindset' (where we believe our talents, abilities and intelligence are set in stone) or a 'growth mindset' (where we believe that with effort and practice we can improve at something).

For example, a child with a fixed mindset when it comes to maths will see their ability in maths as something they were born with. If they are not very good at maths, they will say things like, 'Oh, I'm just not a maths person.' These children will give up easily when they do challenging maths work and will see their mistakes as confirmation that they can't do maths and won't ever be good at it. Even if they are good at maths, these children will think they just 'get' maths and don't necessarily need to try hard at it. They often try to hide their mistakes (which contradict their self-belief about their innate ability in maths) and are driven by a fear of failure, rather than a love of the subject. In the fixed mindset, pupils seem preoccupied with how they will be judged. They fixate on performance and guard against the risk of failure by avoiding opportunities to learn if they know they will make mistakes (Nussbaum and Dweck, 2008). Children with a fixed mindset tend to stay very firmly in their comfort zone, not wanting to take risks or make mistakes.

In contrast, take the child who has a growth mindset when it comes to maths. They see maths lessons as an opportunity to learn and grow. Whether their current ability in maths is low or high, they say things like, 'I can't do this yet but I'm going to practise to get better.' If they come up against a challenging problem they enjoy getting stuck in and trying different solutions. If they get answers wrong, they don't hide their mistakes but seek out advice and help on where they went wrong, they correct their mistakes or adapt their problem-solving strategy (Blackwell et al., 2007). These pupils increase their efforts when they encounter a setback and they don't give up easily (Nussbaum and Dweck, 2008). Children with a growth mindset tend to inhabit the stretch zone. They seek out challenges, they embrace their mistakes and they enjoy the thrill of being outside their comfort zone.

Clearly, helping children develop a growth mindset is good for their learning, as it encourages them to spend more time in the stretch zone where they learn the most. But how exactly do you help foster a growth mindset in children?

Teaching about the brain

It turns out that teaching children about the plastic nature of their brains goes a long way in helping develop a growth mindset. In one study, two groups of pupils around the age of 12, who were all doing badly in maths, were randomly assigned to workshops on study skills. The control group received standard study skills lessons. The second group were essentially given a mini course in neuroscience. They were taught about the malleability of the brain, how intelligence isn't fixed and that our neurons form new connections every time you learn something new. The results were impressive – the maths scores in the neuroscience group improved whilst those in the control group actually got worse (Blackwell et al., 2007). The research shows that teaching pupils about how they can exercise their brains to grow bigger and stronger motivates them to learn (Dweck, 2007).

Praise

How we praise children also has a tremendous impact on whether they go on to develop a fixed or growth mindset. As a parent myself, it feels almost instinctive to say, 'Clever boy!' every time my two-year-old son masters some new skill. But, inadvertently, I may be reinforcing a fixed mindset in him. Dweck's research shows that praising children's intelligence is more likely to develop a fixed mindset and undermine their resilience (Dweck, 2007). When children are praised for being 'clever', it can actually make them less likely to attempt new challenges because any mistakes they make will conflict with this view their parent or teacher has of them. They are more likely to work in their comfort zone attempting work they know they can do and score highly on, thus upholding the image that they are 'intelligent'.

However, when children are praised for the effort they put in, or their determination or persistence with a challenge, they are much more likely to learn more and perform better. This is known as 'process praise' (i.e. praise for focus, resilience, improvement, strategies, etc.) and, according to the ICEP, 'puts students in a growth mindset and fosters hardy motivation.' (Institute of Child Education and Psychology, Module 3, p. 19) Dweck believes that process praise lets pupils know what they have done to be successful in their learning and what they need to do to be successful in the future (Dweck, 2007).

Tal Ben-Shahar would agree that we need to be mindful about what we praise. Schools tend to focus on praising and rewarding achievements such as high grades in tests or passing exams. The problem with this, according to Ben-Shahar, is that, 'In emphasizing achievements (which are tangible) over the cultivation of a love of learning (which is intangible), schools simultaneously reinforce the rat-race mentality and stifle children's emotional development.' (Ben-Shahar, 2008, p. 85) So, schools and teachers need to take heed. If we want to develop a growth mindset in our children, where they are more willing to step inside the stretch zone, embrace challenges, and learn to love learning, praising the process rather than the end result may be the best way to achieve this.

The mouse in the maze

Part of the challenge for the teacher is encouraging children to leave their comfort zones. If their mindset is particularly fixed, it can be hard to convince them that making mistakes and doing work that they will struggle at is good for their development! Therefore, *how* you present work and challenges in your classroom is vitally important. In their book, *Mindfulness*, Mark Williams and Danny Penman share an experiment that was carried out at the University of Maryland involving a mouse in a maze (Williams and Penman, 2011, pp. 112–14). Two groups of pupils were asked to navigate a cartoon mouse through a maze with a slight difference in the puzzles presented. One group had a maze with a delicious-looking piece of cheese awaiting the mouse at the exit. This is known as a 'positive', or 'approach-oriented' puzzle. The second group had no cheese in the maze but, instead, there was a predatory owl ready to swoop and gobble the mouse up at any moment. This is known as a 'negative', or 'avoidant-oriented' puzzle. Both groups solved the puzzles easily in around two minutes but the after-effects of the puzzles were very revealing. After completing the maze puzzle, all pupils were asked to complete an apparently unrelated test that measured creativity. Williams and Penman noted, 'When they did these, those who had avoided the owl did 50 per cent *worse* than those who'd helped the mouse find the cheese.' (Williams and Penman, 2011, p. 113)

It transpired that avoidance triggered the fear instinct in the first group of pupils. Their minds' 'aversion' pathways were activated leaving them feeling vigilant and cautious. They became less creative when operating from a place of fear and avoidance. But the pupils helping the mouse find the cheese had the complete opposite effect. They became more open to new experiences, were more relaxed, playful and eager to experiment. The lack of fear meant they became more open-minded. All of this leads Williams and Penman to the important conclusion that, 'The spirit in which you do something is often as important as the act itself.' (Williams and Penman, 2011, p. 114)

With this in mind, it is vital that teachers use the stretch zone in the class-room in a positive way. Not only can teachers make working in the stretch zone sound exciting and appealing, but they can also make the fear of failure or making mistakes seem less scary. This is why having a safe and secure classroom environment for your tribe, like the ones we explored in Chapter 1 (p. 11), is so important for giving children the confidence to step outside their comfort zones. Cozolino points out that, 'A secure classroom allows students to cope with the stress of new learning and to regulate their fear of failure with the support of their teachers and fellow students.' (Cozolino, 2013, p. 82) A mindfulness practice also gives your pupils a tool for processing, and being with the sometimes uncomfortable feelings of putting themselves in the stretch zone and leaving their place of comfort.

In action

Unless teachers can encourage children to leave their comfort zones and take risks, limited growth and learning will take place. The stretch zone can act as a great metaphor that enables children to push themselves and start to fulfil their true potential. It works most effectively when teachers walk the walk and model what risk-taking looks like by experimenting in the classroom, sharing their own mistakes and trying new things (like writing a book! Arrgggh!). The following activities will help you bring the stretch zone to life so more children inhabit this zone more of the time, and experience the thrill of taking risks.

Stretch zone display

The first thing I do to introduce the stretch zone is teach my first mini neuroscience lesson (see Chapter 4, p. 68–9). This teaches the children that their brains have a huge capacity to learn new things and improve at any task with effort and practice. That lesson definitely helps foster a growth mindset. You could then try the following:

- Create a 'stretch zone' display in your classroom (see Figure 5.3). It needs a comfort zone in the middle (with phrases like 'Easy', 'Know it already', 'Boring'), and then a stretch zone outside (with phrases such as 'Hard', 'Tricky', 'Make mistakes', 'Exciting', 'Fun' and 'Flow'). You don't have to include a panic zone but I would certainly talk about it in relation to the other zones of learning.

- You can download a 'stretch zone' display banner using this link: **www.teachappy.co.uk/resources-and-downloads**.

- Explain that the comfort zone is a place where we know what we're doing. It feels nice there because the work is fairly easy and we don't feel stressed because the work isn't challenging. The comfort zone is a nice place to be, but if we spend too much time there we start to get bored. It might be good to get the children to identify work or activities that are currently in their comfort zones.

- Communicate to your class that when they step outside of their comfort zone, they enter the stretch zone! Here, they'll encounter tricky work. The tasks will be hard, and they may leave them confused and they will definitely make mistakes. In fact, making mistakes is a good sign that they're in the stretch zone! However, if they really focus in the stretch zone, try their best and don't give up, they start to be able to do work that they couldn't do before. It can feel really fun in the stretch zone and exciting when they're able to do something difficult that they could not do before!

Figure 5.3: A 'stretch zone' display with brain goals attached

- Explain that their brain grows the most when they work in the stretch zone, as their neurons fire and wire together! They will even start to experience a state called 'flow' which is where they become so absorbed in their work that time rushes by and they don't think about anything else (see Chapter 6 for more on 'flow', p. 93).

- Get the children to share activities inside and outside school that are in their stretch zone (e.g. speaking in front of an audience, doing backstroke in the pool, using watercolours in art).

- Finally, collect the children's brain goals from your neuroscience lesson and put these up on the 'stretch zone' display. Remind your class that working towards their brain goals will put the children in their stretch zone.

The idea is to get the children excited about being in the stretch zone. You want to make it sound appealing, challenging and absorbing. Whenever you see children challenging themselves, struggling with work and persisting, praise them for working in the stretch zone!

Tales from the classroom

Team Monet was about to go on their first ever residential trip. Everyone was extremely excited, but one anxious parent took me to one side after school to tell me that her daughter, Sarah, might have a problem with sleeping away from home. Just two weeks before our trip, Sarah had to be collected from a friend's house at 2am because she got so upset about being away from home. 'It'll be fine,' I reassured. 'We'll take good care of her.' After a great first day building dens in the woods and tackling an obstacle course, as predicted, on the first night away, Sarah was up late at night in floods of tears. She wanted to go home. Myself and the other members of staff calmed Sarah down and asked her what her favourite part of the first day was. 'I loved den building,' she replied, starting to smile. We chatted about the exciting things we had lined up tomorrow until Sarah felt relaxed and safe. 'You know, staying away from home can be scary at first. But it gets easier,' I explained. 'If you just slept at home all the time, that would be like staying in your comfort zone. It feels nice and safe, which is great, but it can be really fun to step inside your stretch zone and have a sleepover with your friends. So, this trip and staying away from your home is the stretch zone for you. It can feel a bit scary, but I promise you, you'll feel very proud of yourself if you stay.' Reluctantly, Sarah nodded as we took her back to her room. We didn't hear any more from Sarah that night – it was gone midnight and she just conked out. After another fun day exploring the woods, and having fun with her friends, the next night was interesting. As the children got into their bunk beds, Sarah called out, 'Mr Bethune!'

'Yes?' I replied.

'I feel sad it's our last day tomorrow. I don't want to go home – I'm having too much fun!' Sarah said, beaming.

Beautiful mistakes

A key facet of the stretch zone and growth mindset is about communicating to children that mistakes and failure are a key part of learning and growth. Too often children view mistakes as a sign that they aren't good at something and that they never will be. Mistakes can demoralise some children and force them to give up and retreat back to their comfort zones. It is crucial that teachers create a classroom environment in which mistakes are shared, talked about and celebrated. Why not try the following?

- Host a 'share a mistake' part of your lessons when children volunteer to share with the class a mistake they have made. They either share it and ask the class for help, with other children then assisting with correcting the mistake. Alternatively, they could share the mistake they made and also how they corrected it themselves.

- You could also have a 'mistake of the week' where you put up a maths problem, or a passage of writing with mistakes that the children have to identify and solve. Children could put up their various solutions on sticky notes, particularly if the problem or mistake has more than one solution.

- When you inevitably make mistakes in your teaching be sure to share these with the children. Not only does this show humility but also it models that mistakes happen to everyone and there is no need to be ashamed of them.

Creating a culture where mistakes are valued helps the children realise that mistakes are actually essential for learning and that if we share them with others, we all get to learn from those mistakes.

'Flearning'

A powerful way to encourage children to put themselves in the stretch zone is by showing them their role models stretching themselves, embracing challenges and making mistakes. Our school had a visit from BMX superstar Mike Mullen. Mike is a former World Masterclass BMX Champion and current UK Pro Halfpipe Champion. He runs BMX Academy (**www.bmxacademy.com**), which teaches growth mindset through BMX. In his assembly to the children, he shared his story about how he went from an anxious, worried schoolboy to BMX champion. Mike explained how he had a fixed mindset at school and believed he simply wasn't good at certain things. It was only when he got a BMX for his birthday that he started practising tricks.

At first, he couldn't do them and would keep failing. But, unlike at school, Mike kept persevering with mastering his BMX tricks. He realised that every time he failed, he learned something new about what to do to get better at the trick. Eventually, through repeated failure and continued learning, Mike mastered the tricks! He then coined the phrase 'failure + learning = Flearning'. The children were so inspired by his message, that 'flearning' has now become a catchphrase in our school when we make a mistake.

It can be so inspiring to invite people from the top of their field to come and share their stories of success and failure with the children. But even if this is not possible, you can share the many stories of successful people whose journeys are littered with mistakes and failure. Basketball player, Michael Jordan, was dropped from his school basketball team because he wasn't good enough. Not only did he go on to be the most successful basketball player of all time, but he shares this message about his success: 'I've missed more than 9,000 shots in my career. I've lost almost 300 games. 26 times, I've been trusted to take the game winning shot and missed. I've failed over and over…And *that* is why I succeed.' (Jordan in Goldman and Papson, 1999, p. 49) Similarly, J. K. Rowling, author of the *Harry Potter* books, says this about her experience of failure: 'I had failed on an epic scale. An exceptionally short-lived marriage had imploded, and I was jobless, a lone parent, and as poor as it is possible to be in modern Britain, without being homeless.' (Rowling, 2008) Clearly this didn't stop her and Rowling went on to be the author of the best-selling book series in the history of literature!

Be like the penguin

But sometimes children don't like the feeling of making mistakes and they do want to give up in the stretch zone. Which is why I also show my class a brilliant clip from the BBC's *Planet Earth* series, available here: **www.bbc.co.uk/programmes/p0014qkz**. The clip shows a gentoo penguin trying to escape from a sea lion. The sea lion is faster

Figure 5.4: A focused table gets the penguin toy

and stronger than the penguin on land and it manages to capture it in its jaws twice. But both times the penguin keeps fighting and struggles free. It's a very dramatic clip. I first showed this clip to a Year 2 class and their response was amazing – they whooped, cheered and clapped when the penguin finally escaped back into the sea. The phrase 'Be like the penguin' was born and I use it as a symbol for resilience and perseverance.

Whenever we find something hard and feel like giving up, we remember the penguin, we dig a bit deeper and we keep going. The penguin is a great metaphor for the children because it is the underdog but it triumphs due to its grit and tenacity. I have two stuffed penguin toys in my class (which former pupils bought me as end-of-term presents) and I place them on the tables (see Figure 5.4) where I can see children working in the stretch zone and trying their best. I even have a penguin stamp that I use in books where I can see pupils have really tried to stretch themselves and put in extra effort.

This is one way of giving 'process praise'. By recognising where children have stepped outside of their comfort zone, made mistakes, tried hard, persevered and bounced back, it encourages them to spend more time in the stretch zone. There is an interesting paradox with working in the stretch zone and it is this: the more you step outside of your comfort zone and become familiar with the uncomfortable feelings that often accompany working there, the more comfortable you become with those feelings and so your comfort zone grows! The stretch zone becomes a less scary place to work, it becomes more exciting to be there and so children continue to stretch themselves and grow.

Youcubed.org

Another excellent resource is the **Youcubed.org** content created by Jo Boaler at Stanford University. Although this website contains videos that are designed to change children's mindsets about maths, they perfectly sum up the latest neuroscience in easily digestible ways for children and are relevant to *all* subjects that children learn. I often show these videos in class because they reinforce key messages such as:

- there is no such thing as a 'maths brain' (or an English, or science, or anything brain)
- mistakes grow our brains
- struggling with tricky problems helps grow our brains more (stretch zone!)
- speed is not important in maths (or any subject), but thinking deeply is
- our brains are plastic and grow with practice, persistence and effort
- believing in yourself helps your brain grow more than doubting yourself.

I have found that teaching children about the stretch zone works on many levels. This is not just about helping them do better at their schoolwork. The stretch zone teaches children about how to deal with the inevitable anxiety and stress that comes from modern life. It teaches them that in order to grow and fulfil your potential, you will often have to encounter uncomfortable feelings, face your fears and make mistakes – and that's OK. It works in the classroom, it works on the sports field and it works in any area of their lives where they have some difficult thing to do (e.g. visiting a sick relative, dealing with friendship issues or sticking up for themselves if they face bullying). The stretch zone really does help children develop self-confidence, resilience and perseverance.

Key points

- When learning anything new, children need the right level of challenge, stress and stimulation to engage them.

- The stretch zone provides this sweet spot of challenge but it can feel unnerving for children to leave their comfort zones.

- You may need to change children's mindset from fixed ones (where they believe talent and intelligence is innate) to growth ones (where they believe intelligence and talent is grown and worked at).

- Share with children the different zones of learning and get them to reflect on where they spend most of their time.

- Encourage children to be brave and work more inside the stretch zone by celebrating mistakes, providing a supportive classroom environment and making it exciting to work there.

- Give 'process praise' when you can see them working hard and attempting challenges, and develop their determination and resilience by encouraging them to 'be like the penguin' and by sharing stories of their role models' successes and failures.

Chapter 6
Flow and strengths

May what I do flow from me like a river, no forcing and no holding back, the way it is with children.

– Rainer Maria Rilke

Chapter overview

In this chapter, we'll explore exactly what flow is and why it is vital for our creativity and wellbeing. We will understand how we can cultivate more flow experiences in the classroom and how, by nurturing and tapping into children's strengths, we can help foster a love of learning.

In theory	In action
• What is flow?	• Show me your flow
• Benefits of flow	• Differentiation
• The anti-flow classroom	• Making learning meaningful
• Strengths	• Flow-rich activities
• Strengths in the classroom	• Strength spotting

In theory

What is flow?

Think back to a time in the classroom when you were working at your best. The children were focused and engaged, you were enjoying what you were doing and you were in your element. You would have naturally incorporated your innate strengths into the lesson, maybe utilising your creativity, sharing your love of learning and using timely humour. Time rushed by and you didn't think about anything else other than what you were doing. In moments like these, you would have been experiencing 'flow' – a state of pure concentration and deep satisfaction.

Psychologist Mihaly Csikszentmihalyi (pronounced cheeks-sent-me-high) has extensively researched the concept of flow – a state of mind he discovered whilst researching creativity and productivity. He describes flow as: 'Being completely involved in an activity for its own sake. The ego falls away. Time flies. Every action, movement, and thought follows inevitably from the previous one…Your whole being is involved, and you're using your skills to the utmost.' (Csikszentmihalyi, 2002) Flow experiences are times when we are operating at our highest levels and reaching our full potential. It occurs when we are deeply absorbed and engaged in something. People often describe it as 'being in the zone', which is why it is so closely related to working in the stretch zone (see Chapter 5, p. 77). You cannot experience flow if you are either bored or anxious. Similar to the Yerkes-Dodson graph in the previous chapter (p. 79), Figure 6.1 below shows when flow is most likely to be experienced.

Csikszentmihalyi notes that there are certain conditions that need to be in place for us to experience flow:

1. we must engage in a challenging task where the level of challenge matches our level of skill

2. the challenge must be clear and have obvious goals

3. we must get immediate feedback from the task so we know how well we are doing

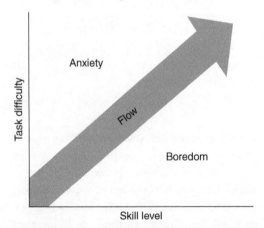

Figure 6.1: A graph showing when flow is experienced

4. we must be able to really focus on the task in hand

5. we should have a sense of autonomy over our actions in relation to the task.

Although experiencing flow mainly happens when working in the stretch zone, they are not the same thing. Let me illustrate the difference with a personal example. Writing this book is definitely putting me in the stretch zone. I have never written a book before so I'm out of my comfort zone, I'm making mistakes and I'm learning lots. Very often, I experience flow whilst writing. There are times when I'm so absorbed in writing that, before I know it, the afternoon has arrived and I haven't eaten lunch, had a drink or gone to the loo since the morning! After being in flow, I feel great. I look back and realise how much I enjoyed writing, and I feel satisfied and can't wait to start again. However, there are also times when I have been stuck for ideas, or received some critical feedback, or I've read back my work and disliked it. At these times, I'm not in flow but I am still in the stretch zone. I have to dig deep, keep going and push through the difficult feelings until I can find my rhythm again. As Ken Robinson writes in his book, *The Element*, 'Doing the thing you love is no guarantee you'll be in the zone every time. Sometimes the mood isn't right, the time is wrong, and the ideas just don't flow.' (Robinson, 2010, pp. 88–9)

There are also different levels of flow that we might experience. We might enjoy the 'micro-flow' of an engrossing conversation with a friend, or getting lost in a good book. But, we can also experience really deep flow when all of our strengths, talents and faculties are being tested to their limits. This description by world-famous cellist, Yo-Yo Ma, gives us an insight into how deep flow feels: 'I…turn off that part of the mind that judges everything. I'm not thinking or worrying…It's when I'm least conscious of what I'm doing, when I'm lost in the emotion of the music, that I'm performing at my best.' (Lehrer, 2012, p. 89)

Benefits of flow

Flow doesn't just feel good, it does us good too. Studies show that being in flow is strongly associated with happiness and wellbeing. When he tracked 500 teenagers in one study, Csikszentmihalyi found that the 'high-flow' teenagers (those who experienced flow on a regular basis) had more hobbies, were involved in more sports and did more homework than the 'low-flow' children (those who rarely experienced flow). Interestingly, the high-flow teenagers didn't always report that their higher levels of engagement were fun or enjoyable at the time, but their experience of flow paid off later down the line. It turned out that the high-flow teenagers scored more highly on measures of psychological wellbeing, were more likely to go to university, had stronger social ties and were ultimately happier and more successful (Csikszentmihalyi, 2002).

Pupil engagement and experiences of flow in school is also strongly correlated with academic performance. Additional research by Csikszentmihalyi and colleagues shows that flow deepens learning and encourages long-term interest in a subject. This stands to reason. Every teacher knows that children who are engaged in lessons learn better than those who aren't. Flow experiences in the classroom really help children develop a love of learning, which is surely one of the key aims of any primary school teacher. When children are turned on to learning, they can really start to reach their full potential both academically and emotionally.

The anti-flow classroom

One of the challenges teachers face, however, is that schools are often set up in such a way that make flow experiences hard to achieve. American psychologist, Jill Suttie, claims that, 'The learning conditions in classrooms have been practically antithetical to the conditions people need to achieve flow and all the benefits that come with it.' She points the finger at high-stakes testing and over-regimentation in classrooms, saying it is 'making it harder for students to get deeply engaged with topics that interest them.' When you have an education system that values academic achievement over pupil engagement, Suttie claims children start to disengage and burn out as they don't see the point in what they are learning. Alarmingly, when researchers at Harvard and Villanova universities studied high-achieving pupils at secondary schools in America, they found that the feeling of needing to achieve, in the absence of true pupil engagement in learning, was associated with 'cheating, sleepless nights, depression, and drug abuse.' (Suttie, 2012)

Educational expert, Sir Ken Robinson, agrees that schools often stifle creativity and the experience of flow in the process. He believes that creativity in schools should be given equal status to core subjects like

English. But he realises that many schools do the complete opposite of this. Robinson argues: 'We're now running national education systems where mistakes are the worst thing you can make. And the result is that we are educating people out of their creative capacities.' (Robinson, 2006) Csikszentmihalyi also thinks a lot of schools generally make learning dull and uninteresting. He believes, 'Schools generally fail to teach how exciting, how mesmerizingly beautiful science or mathematics can be; they teach the routine of literature or history rather than the adventure.' (Csikszentmihalyi, 1998)

Teachers need to be mindful of the constraints of the system that they are working within, but there is still lots they can do to create more flow-rich experiences in the classroom and one way is to focus on children's strengths.

Strengths

Our strengths are core parts of ourselves and they shape our personalities. They are what drive our thoughts, feelings and behaviours and, ultimately, they are what motivate us. Positive psychologist Vanessa King says that, 'When we're using our strengths, we tend to enjoy what we're doing more, learn easily and do better.' (King, 2016, p. 191) When we use our strengths we feel energised rather than burnt out. According to strengths expert, Martin Seligman, using your strengths is essential in experiencing flow. He states: 'There are no shortcuts to flow…you need to deploy your highest strengths and talents to meet the world in flow.' (Seligman, 2011, p. 11) Therefore, tapping into children's strengths in the classroom can be a key tool in motivating them and engaging them in learning.

But what are the different types of strengths? Seligman and psychologist Christopher Peterson have identified 24 universal character strengths and virtues summarised in Figure 6.2.

They have been grouped under the six virtues: courage; wisdom and knowledge; humanity; justice, temperance; and transcendence. Seligman argues that each of us have several 'signature strengths' which we will use more than others and when we use them in our work and play, we are often at our happiest (Seligman, 2002). Indeed, when participants in one study were asked to identify their top five strengths and actively use one of them in a new way for a week, they were significantly happier up to six months later (Seligman et al., 2005).

Figure 6.2: The 24 character strengths identified by Seligman and Peterson (Seligman et al., 2005)

Strengths in the classroom

One of the challenges with strengths is identifying them in ourselves. Because they are innate to us, we can easily overlook them or take them for granted. Therefore, teachers are key in helping children identify their character strengths and making them explicit. Praising a child for their 'persistence' or 'teamwork' helps them acknowledge that strength in themselves, which in turn builds self-confidence. This has the knock-on effect of encouraging that child to take risks and step into their stretch zone. Teachers can create a classroom culture of identifying strengths, where the children also start to identify strengths in each other.

Children have the capacity to develop all 24 strengths and virtues but some are more prevalent in childhood than others. For instance, very young children tend to display the strengths of love, kindness, creativity, curiosity and humour (Park and Peterson, 2006). Other strengths such as perspective, prudence and appreciation of beauty tend to be more common in adults. The ICEP warns against teaching children the strengths that adults value over their innate values and they state, 'We need to be careful to nurture the strengths they already possess, otherwise they may lose them as they mature.' (Institute of Child Education and Psychology, Module 3, p. 21) The aim is not to limit children to their core, signature strengths but to allow them to develop, practise and cultivate the full spectrum of their strengths.

An important point to note is that many studies show that strengths of the 'heart', such as love and gratitude, are more strongly associated with wellbeing than strengths of the 'head', like critical thinking or leadership (Park and Peterson, 2009). There is a strong case for focusing more on the former, if we truly want to teach children the skills of happiness. In Chapter 7, we'll look at some great ways to develop strengths of the heart like kindness, empathy and compassion (p. 111).

In action

By giving children more experiences of flow in the classroom, and by helping them develop their strengths, teachers can really start to help pupils reach their full potential. When pupils are fully engaged in their learning and using the best parts of themselves to work, you really start to see them flourish. Schoolwork no longer becomes a chore or tiresome, it becomes a joy – a source of both pleasure and purpose.

Show me your flow

A simple activity to get children to think about flow, what it feels like and when they experience it is to get them to share with the class their favourite flow activities. Ask your class:

- What are the things they love to do at home or school where they experience flow? (i.e. what activities do they get lost in where time rushes by and they lose sense of themselves?)

- Get them to discuss as a class what it feels like to be in flow.

- Individually, they could create a poster, drawing and writing about their top five flow activities, and present these to the class. Identify if there are any common themes (are they mainly sports related, arts and crafts based, inside or outside school?) and notice if their flow activities tend to be ones they do on their own, in a group or a mixture of both.

When we experience flow, we are often using some of our signature strengths.

- Can the children identify what signature strengths they might be using when they are performing their flow activities? Maybe 'focus' when playing an instrument, or 'love of learning' when reading a book, or 'joy' when playing games with their friends.

The key is to get children more familiar with the concept of flow, noticing when they experience it the most, and what strengths they might be using. This helps them realise that by choosing to do an activity where they experience flow, they have the ability to boost their wellbeing.

Differentiation

One of the key preconditions for children experiencing flow, is that the challenge of the task must match the skill of the child. This is normally done through differentiation in the classroom and requires teachers knowing their children really well. Here are three of the ways you could differentiate work in your classroom (although this is by no means an exhaustive list):

- **By task**: In this scenario, you provide different tasks that the children could complete depending on their skill level. Some schools use a 'chilli' system, where work is rated as 'mild', 'medium', or 'hot' chilli. By allowing the pupil to select the work they feel matches their skill level, it affords them autonomy in getting to exercise choice (another key ingredient in experiencing flow). If they start on the 'mild' task, they can always move up to the 'medium' and 'hot' tasks later, increasing the challenge as they go. Be mindful of those children who choose to remain in their comfort zones by selecting work they know they can do. By encouraging children to step into the stretch zone, it nudges them to choose work where they will make mistakes but the challenge keeps them in that sweet spot of arousal.

- **By support**: Teachers can give every child the same task or challenge but may give more assistance, feedback and support to children depending on their needs. By giving support, you can guide and encourage pupils whilst also creating a safe space so they can cope with the struggle they'll experience on the task. You're also on hand to praise their effort and persistence, which helps them identify strengths and fosters a growth mindset. The key is not to always assist the same children, otherwise they may become overly reliant on adult support, so mix up who you work with. Your aim is to stretch the children and to grow their independence.

- **By outcome**: Here you set the same task but every child will produce different outcomes depending on their skill level. One really good way to do this is to provide them with 'low floor, high ceiling' tasks. These are tasks where each pupil can access it at their level. So, the 'low floor' allows pupils new to the subject to find the right level of challenge for them and those pupils who are more experienced can go much deeper with their thinking, and aim for the 'high ceiling'. These tasks are often open-ended investigations and with more than one 'right answer'. In fact, sometimes there are no 'right answers' at all, just the opportunity for children to discuss, debate, experiment and explore.

Making learning meaningful

Another key facet of flow-rich classrooms is that the challenge or task must have clear and obvious goals. Now, I'm certainly not a teacher who recommends having a learning objective for every single lesson, along with very prescriptive success criteria. I believe this can sometimes hinder creativity and hamper flow. However, children do need to know what the point of the task is that you are asking them to complete. When children know what the challenge involves and what the goals are, they are then able to lose themselves in the task and are more likely to experience flow. So, when any challenge or task is set, make sure you set clear and understandable goals (one to three maximum) that the class can work towards.

Furthermore, to engage pupils in their schoolwork even more, it really helps if they know how the work is relevant to their lives. You can either:

- Make it clear during a lesson how the learning is relevant to them (e.g. improving mental addition can help you when you're out shopping and need to know if you can afford some items, or to check you've been given the correct change).

- Or, you can get the children to work out how the learning is relevant to them. A study that got low-performing science students to write about how a lesson was relevant to their lives showed they had more interest in the subject and got higher grades than those students who didn't do the writing task (Hulleman and Harackiewicz, 2009).

- Finally, if you are teaching something that neither you nor the children can see the point of, maybe you could use your time more wisely to teach something more relevant and valuable.

Flow-rich activities

Here are three activities to try with your class to help you and them experience more flow in their learning:

1. Debates

I love a good philosophy debate in class and they are often a great way to experience flow. They are inclusive, everyone can join in, and they can take many twists and turns. They help develop children's reasoning and oracy skills. Here is how you can do it:

- Start by having a stimulus to generate open questions they'd like to debate. The stimulus could be an object, a short film clip or a picture book.

- In groups, the children then come up with an open question they'd like to discuss based on the stimulus (examples of previous questions my classes have debated are: Why do we have to go to school? Why do we need money? Is it ever OK to break the law?). Each group chooses their favourite question and the teacher scribes these on the board.

- Once you have about five or six questions on the board, everyone in the class then votes for the question they'd like to debate. The question with the most votes wins. In doing so, you've also introduced your class to democracy – its benefits ('Yay, I got to debate my question!') and its pitfalls ('Boo! I didn't want that!').

- Once the debate gets going, your role as teacher is not to get involved too much. Encourage the quieter children to have their say. See if children can take the role of devil's advocate (intentionally finding faults in others' arguments). Definitely encourage respectful arguing – 'I disagree with David's point because…' rather than 'Err, that's a rubbish point, Dave!'

- If a question runs its course, simply move on to debate the next most popular question. If your first debate doesn't go so well, don't be disheartened – it can take a few attempts before your class get into the flow of debating, as it is likely to be a new skill they are learning.

Tales from the classroom

It was the last morning lesson before lunch and we were having a philosophical debate in Year 4. The question we had voted to discuss was, 'What happens to us after we die?' I am always amazed at the innate wisdom of young children. The debate moved from pragmatic and practical arguments ('We stop breathing, our bodies start to decay and the worms eat us'), to metaphysical ones ('If the worms eat us, they get our energy, so we live on and we never really die'). This particular debate had lots of energy and everyone was getting involved. There were arguments and counter-arguments. There was a real a buzz in the room as the debate got going. But then Nancy put her hand up. 'I think we're in flow, Mr Bethune.'

'How do you know?' I asked.

'Because it's 12.05pm and we're late for lunch.'

The class quickly filed out to lunch, debating as they went, and a few lingered behind to convince me of their lines of thinking. It doesn't happen often that your pupils don't want to go to lunch, but when it does, and they're in flow, it feels so good.

2. The beauty of maths

Maths professor Jo Boaler has worked closely with Carol Dweck to try to change the way teachers, children and parents view maths. Rather than it being viewed as a dry subject, mainly about calculations with right and wrong answers, Boaler has created a three-week course for primary school children to show them the creativity, beauty and imagination of maths. The lessons have useful plans, resources and extension tasks, which means for three whole weeks you don't need to plan a maths lesson as Jo Boaler and her team have done it for you!

I have taught the 'Inspirational Maths' lessons to several classes and they really do help turn on all children to maths and help them realise that maths is not just about numbers! In these lessons I, and the children, really do experience flow, as we get stuck into interesting investigations. The focus is on group work, and children working collaboratively in teams to help prove points and argue their case (very similar to the skills used in debating). Go to **www.youcubed.org/week-of-inspirational-math** to sign up to the free resources and get your children exploring maths in a new and engaging way.

3. Design and technology

From my experience, children often experience flow when drawing, designing and making things. The James Dyson Foundation has created some excellent free 'challenges' for primary schools to help children understand and experience the design and engineering process. Why not try the 'spaghetti bridge challenge'? Here is how you do it:

- Give the children their 'brief', which is to design and build a bridge to support the weight of a 250g bag of sugar.
- Hand out the raw materials of spaghetti, masking tape and sticky tack.
- The resource card from Dyson gives the children some design ideas but, really, it's over to them to design and test their bridges.
- Don't over teach this. Let the children explore the brittleness of their raw materials. Let them experiment with how to stick it all together. Let them fail, then redesign, fail again and redesign again!

- Finally, test the bridges and get the children to evaluate each other's designs.

This is a great lesson. It is easy to show the relevance of the learning because what the children are doing is basically the design process that any object in the classroom or their house would have gone through before being manufactured. Be prepared for lots of spaghetti to clear up at the end though! Go to **www.jamesdysonfoundation.co.uk/resources/challenge-cards** for more ideas and to download your free pack of 'Challenge cards'.

Strength spotting

It is likely that your children will be unfamiliar with some of the 24 character strengths. Therefore, you will need to teach children what strengths are, what they look like in action and give them opportunities to spot their own and their classmates' strengths. Here are some ways to bring strengths to life in the classroom:

- A great video to show to your class, that explains what character strengths are and how we can grow them, is called 'The Science of Character' (**www.letitripple.org/films/science-of-character**).

- It can also help to have a display in your classroom listing the 24 character strengths so your children become more familiar with them. One of the best online resources is the VIA Character Strengths website (**www.viacharacter.org/www/Character-Strengths**), which gives a short description of each strength. They also have great visual character strengths icons, which you could enlarge, print out and have on display: **www.viacharacter.org/www/Portals/0/Character%20Strength%20Icons%20NEW%20FINAL2.pdf**.

- Children in Years 5 and 6 could even take the VIA Character Strengths Youth Survey online (aimed at ten- to 17-year-olds: **www.viacharacter.org/survey/account/register**). It is free and takes about 15 minutes to complete, and the children will need an email address. The survey will identify their top five signature strengths.

- At the start of some lessons, you could identify three strengths that you would like the class to use during the task. If they're working in groups on a problem-solving challenge, for example, you might select 'teamwork', 'perseverance' and 'creativity'. When you notice children displaying those strengths, you simply acknowledge it and praise them. If you see anyone using other strengths, notice and praise those too. By getting into the habit of noticing and praising strengths in your pupils, not only is it another way to counteract their natural 'negativity bias' but it also models to the class that we all have things we are good at, and it's good to point those things out.

- A lovely activity to help children spot strengths in each other is to give each child a class list of everyone's names and an empty box next to each name. They have to take each name and think of one strength that that child has displayed with an example and then write it down in a sentence in the box. For example, 'Mo – shows kindness when he lets other children join in with his games' or 'Sinita – showed bravery when she stuck up for me at netball club.' The teacher collects these in and cuts up the names and sentences into strips. All of the sentences that are about Mo get collected and stuck onto his sheet, and the same for Sinita and every other child. Laminate the sheets and then present each child with their strengths sheet. It can be an extremely positive experience for a child to be shown the strengths that others have spotted in them. I bet some of them they never knew they had!

Superhero in you

As well as others spotting strengths in us, it is important that we develop the skill of identifying strengths in ourselves. A fun way to do this is to carry out the following 'superhero in you' exercise:

- Give each child a blank superhero template with their own headshot photo stuck on (see Figure 6.3). You can download the superhero template using this link: **www.teachappy.co.uk/ resources-and-downloads**.

- Tell children that strengths are like superpowers that we have inside of ourselves. If you haven't done so already, show them the 'Science of Character' video (see p. 105).

- Get them to think of their top three strengths (if they struggle with this, they could choose the three they'd most like to have, or a friend could spot strengths in them) and write these next to their superhero figure. They can then give their superhero a name and design a colourful outfit.

● The next part is to then create a comic strip called 'At My Best' (you can download the comic strip template here: **www.teachappy. co.uk/resources-and-downloads**). Using their superhero figure, they create a short story comic strip about how they have used their superpower strengths to good effect (see Figure 6.4). The comic strip

Figure 6.3: A superhero figure 'Captain Cakes' whose strengths are humour, determination and kindness

Figure 6.4: The comic strip showing 'Captain Cakes' putting his strengths into action

can be fiction or they could write about a real-life situation when they used their strengths.

- The children can then present their 'At My Best' comic strip story to the class. This is a fun and engaging way for children to think about their own strengths and how they can apply them in the real world. It teaches children that when we use our strengths we often perform at our best, and doing so helps us experience flow, as well as making us feel happier.

Role models

Sometimes, children (and adults!) have a hard time recognising their strengths. For whatever reason, they simply aren't able to identify what they're good at or what strengths of character they have. Some people argue that the role models we choose to aspire to actually have the character strengths and qualities we possess but which we are too humble or short-sighted to recognise. Therefore, using this role model activity in class can be a good way to develop their strengths:

- Ask the children to choose one role model who they admire from books, TV or films. It can be a fictional character like Harry Potter, or a real-life person such as J. K. Rowling. Maybe they could print off a photo of their role model.

- They then think of what their role model's top three character strengths are and list these next to their picture.

- Ask the children to think about how their role model uses their strengths and what they can learn from this. Do their strengths benefit society at all and, if so, how?

- Children could end the task by thinking about how they can develop the strengths that their role model has. For example, if their role model shows kindness, maybe they could choose to do more acts of kindness in school by helping tidy up in class, or inviting children to join their games at playtime.

Even if they've chosen someone famous for their looks, or (heaven forbid) a reality-TV star, shifting the focus onto that person's character strengths avoids focusing on superficial qualities such as having nice hair, a pretty face, or for simply 'being famous'.

Key points

- Flow is a state of mind when we are completely absorbed in an activity. We lose sense of ourselves, time rushes by and we are using our skills and strengths to meet the challenges of the task. Flow is associated with higher levels of happiness and an improved ability to learn.

- We often experience flow when we use our strengths. Our strengths are the core parts of ourselves that shape our personalities and drive us. People report higher levels of wellbeing when they use their strengths in daily life.

- Teachers can actively create the classroom conditions that are conducive to flow such as:
  - differentiating work so the challenge of the task matches the skill of the child
  - giving children choice in the work they are completing
  - setting clear goals and making work relevant to children

- allowing them to focus on work completely and lose themselves in the task
- ensuring pupils get feedback from the task, each other or the teacher.

- Provide fun and engaging lessons where children get to debate big ideas, discover the beauty in maths and design, build and create.
- Create a classroom culture of spotting children's strengths. Praise children when they use different strengths and encourage them to spot strengths in each other.
- Encourage children to identify their own 'superhero' strengths and when they have used them to be 'at their best'. Use role models to spot strengths and identify how we can cultivate those strengths too.

Chapter 7
It's cool to be kind

You can always, always give something even if it's a simple act of kindness!

– Anne Frank

Chapter overview

In this chapter, we'll delve into the science of kindness. We'll look at why we are hardwired to be kind, and how kindness positively affects our health and levels of happiness. Finally, we will learn novel ways to develop the strength of kindness in children.

In theory	In action
• Hardwired to be kind	• It's cool to be kind week
• Benefits of kindness	• Class acts of kindness
• The virtuous circle	• Good deed feed
• Cultivating kindness	• Fundraising
	• Befriending meditation

In theory

Hardwired to be kind

In this chapter, I will refer to empathy, kindness, altruism and compassion. They are similar but all slightly different. Let me explain. Empathy is the ability to sense other people's emotions and think about what others may be thinking or feeling. Kindness is a general term that means being friendly, helpful and generous towards others (psychologists often call it 'prosocial' behaviour). Altruism is when we act to promote someone else's welfare even at a risk or cost to ourselves. Compassion is the ability to sense another's suffering and then feeling compelled to try to relieve their suffering.

There is growing evidence that compassion and kindness are hardwired into our DNA because it was essential to our survival as a species. We learned in Chapter 1 (p. 16) that Charles Darwin's theory of human evolution noted that communities that were the most kind and sympathetic to one another, flourished the best and raised the most children. Similarly, our 'social brain' means we need to connect and cooperate with others to help our development. Other studies show that mothers' brains are wired to experience positive emotions when bonding with their children (Nitschke et al., 2004). When a mother is kind, loving and caring towards her baby, it feels good because it does her and her baby good.

Cozolino also notes that in the early 20th century, doctors couldn't work out why children in orphanages had such high mortality rates. Believing infections were to blame, doctors separated children from one another and kept handling by adults to a minimum to reduce infections spreading. Despite these rules, mortality rates remained alarmingly high. It was only when attachment researchers suggested that children be held and played with by consistent caregivers and allowed to interact with one another, that their survival rates improved (Cozolino, 2013, p. 4, citing Blum, 2002). To be loved and cared for actually helps to keep us alive.

But humans' hardwiring for kindness goes beyond the parent–child relationship and extends to others too. When people help unrelated others, neurons in the reward and pleasure centres of the brain are firing away (Rilling et al., 2002). When our brain's reward centres are active, it is nature's way of saying to us, 'This feels good. Do this again.' Even babies' brains are wired to be attracted to kind others. In his book, *A Force For Good,* emotional intelligence expert, Dan Goleman, relays a novel experiment in which babies were shown a cartoon of three shapes: a circle, a square and a triangle, each with large cute eyes. In the cartoon, the circle struggles to move up a hill, and the kind triangle comes along and gives the circle a helpful push to get to the top. Next, the circle struggles up the hill again, but this time the mean square jumps on it, knocking the circle back down the hill. In the final part of the experiment, the babies, given the choice of toys in the shape of the kind triangle, or mean square, invariably choose the nice one (Goleman, 2015, pp. 50–1).

Cynics may argue that kindness, although hardwired, is still ultimately a selfish act (either by promoting our genes or by making us feel good). But there is evidence that shows that when we are focused on being kind to others, and the reward centres of our brains are firing away, the areas of the brain that are concerned with ourselves and our problems actually quieten down (Lutz et al., 2008). So, by thinking about and helping others, we actually think less about ourselves.

Benefits of kindness

Emerson once said, 'It is one of the most beautiful compensations of this life that no man can sincerely try to help another without helping himself.' Science now backs this up, as numerous studies on kindness and compassion show that they benefit our happiness levels and our health. Let's take a look at these areas:

1. Happiness

As mentioned above, when we partake in kind acts towards others, our brains' reward centres are firing and our bodies release happy hormones like dopamine. These make us feel good and boost our levels of happiness. Vanessa King cites one study of 1,700 female volunteers, where the researchers found that many of the women experienced a 'helpers' high'. This was characterised by a feeling of euphoria after helping others, resulting from a release of endorphins, followed by a longer period of feeling calm, peaceful and serene (King, 2016, p. 17). Similarly, Sonja Lyubomirsky has found that people told to complete five acts of kindness over the course of a day report feeling much happier than the control group, and that the feeling lasts for many days after the exercise is over (Lyubomirsky, 2007, pp. 127–9).

It appears we also get more happiness from spending money on others rather than on ourselves. In an experiment carried out by Professor Elizabeth Dunn, volunteers were given envelopes with either $5 or $20 inside, accompanied by a note. The note either instructed the volunteers to spend the money on themselves or to spend it on someone else (either by buying a gift or donating it to charity). The experiment concluded that, 'Individuals who spent money on others were measurably happier than those who spent money on themselves – even though there were no differences between the two groups at the beginning of the day.' Interestingly, it made no difference whether $5 or $20 was spent – just the act of spending on others boosted happiness levels (Dunn and Norton, 2013, pp. 107–9).

And the link between prosocial spending and happiness is replicated throughout the world. Between 2006 and 2008, more than 200,000 people responded to a Gallup World Poll survey. Some of the questions asked whether they had donated to charity in the last month and how satisfied they were with their lives. In 120 out of 136 countries, people who donated to charity in the last month reported greater life satisfaction (Aknin et al., 2013a). These studies show that doing good feels good.

2. Health

In his book, *The Happiness Advantage*, Shawn Achor explains that a long line of empirical data shows that people who are altruistic towards loved ones and strangers have lower levels of stress and improved mental health (Achor, 2011, p. 52). This may be because when we show kindness towards others, our bodies release the happy hormone, oxytocin (Barraza and Zak, 2009). This powerful hormone can counteract the negative effects of the stress hormone, cortisol, and even improve the health of our hearts (Szeto et al., 2008). Dr David Hamilton in *The Five Side Effects of Kindness* states that oxytocin causes the release of nitric oxide, which helps lower blood pressure, as well as reducing the volume of free radicals in our system (which are responsible for ageing and tissue damage), and reducing inflammation of our cardiovascular system (Hamilton, 2017). All of this from simply being kind!

Being more kind and giving towards others also appears to help us live longer. Studies of older people show that those who give support to a variety of people (such as emotional support to a spouse, or by helping friends, relatives and neighbours), live longer than those who choose not to (Brown et al., 2009). Just the act of caring for something else (even if it isn't a person) seems to have amazing health benefits. In an experiment in an elderly nursing home, researchers gave a potted plant to two groups of residents (Langer and Rodin, 1976). One group was told the nurses would take care of the plant for them, whilst the other group was instructed to care for the plant themselves. On average, the residents who cared for the plant themselves showed improved levels of health and well-being and actually lived longer than those who didn't care for their plant. The researchers in this experiment concluded that when we care for others it increases our sense of agency and control, both of which are fundamental to wellbeing. These studies show that doing good does us good.

The virtuous circle

We hear lots about *vicious* circles in life (one bad event can lead to another and another, and we can get stuck in a rut of bad news and negativity) but we hear very little about *virtuous* circles. But it appears that carrying out acts of kindness creates a virtuous circle of positivity. When we help others, it makes us happier and when we are happier, we tend to help others more (Aknin et al., 2011). And so it continues.

More than that, studies show that kindness is contagious. When people benefit from the kindness of others, they often 'pay it forward' by helping others in return. The ripple effect of kindness means one small act can spread far and wide to people we don't know or haven't even met (Fowler and Christakis, 2010). Fascinatingly, each act of kindness helps promote the release of oxytocin in those who carry it out, those who receive it or even those who just *witness* it happening. As well as the health benefits we receive from oxytocin listed on the previous page, it also helps foster trust and connection between people.

Even just being reminded of kind things we have done in the past allows us to experience 'moral elevation' (the positive feeling of knowing you have done a good deed), which in turn increases our motivation to be kind and increases the likelihood that we will partake in altruistic acts in the future (Schnall and Roper, 2011).

Cultivating kindness

Although humans may be hardwired to be kind and altruistic, we will all vary in how kind we are to others. Some people will naturally give a lot of their time and support to others, whereas other people will appear to be a lot stingier. Various researchers have looked to see which factors affect people's levels of empathy, kindness and compassion, and to learn how we can cultivate more of these important skills. This is what they have discovered:

- **Secure attachment**: It has been found that children who are securely attached to their parents are more likely to be sympathetic and kind towards their peers from as early as three and a half years old, compared to those children who were insecurely attached (Waters et al., 1979). We saw in Chapter 1 that teachers leading tribal classrooms can help foster secure attachment in children (p. 11). Tribal classrooms, where all children feel safe, protected and cared for, may be key in providing a secure base for children to show more kind and prosocial behaviour towards others.

- **Empathy**: Another study looked at how parents responded to their children when they had caused harm (Eisenberg and Fabes, 1990). Some parents reasoned with their children, prompting them to consider the consequences of their actions, and how their actions might have harmed others. They encouraged empathy in their children by getting them to put themselves in another's shoes. Other parents used 'power assertion' in response to harmful behaviour, simply declaring what was right and wrong, and often using anger and physical punishment. The children raised to be more empathic were shown to be better adjusted and more likely to help their peers. Therefore, getting children to reflect on their harmful behaviour at school, and helping them understand how their behaviour affects others, can help increase their empathy and prosocial behaviour.

- **Modelling**: One of the most likely ways that children learn kindness is from witnessing their parents being kind. In a landmark study, psychologists Pearl and Samuel Oliner looked at Germans who had helped rescue Jews during the Nazi Holocaust. One of the strongest predictors of this courageous and extremely altruistic behaviour was the individual's memory of growing up in a family that prioritised kindness and compassion (Oliner, 1999). This is why schools that prioritise kindness and care for others provide the best example for their pupils to follow.

- **Loving–kindness meditation**: Brain research shows that a part of the brain known as the 'insula' is activated when we feel genuine empathy for another person. But studies also show that the insula is activated when we partake in mindfulness meditation and regular practice even helps the insula grow and expand (Williams and Penman, 2011). It appears that mindfulness training may increase our ability to show empathy towards others, a prerequisite for being more compassionate and kind. But a meditation practice often referred to as 'loving-kindness', has been shown to really help cultivate compassion in people (Weng et al., 2013). In a 'loving-kindness' practice, you would typically start by cultivating feelings of kindness towards yourself, then extending these feelings to a loved one, then to a neutral stranger, then to someone whom you find difficult and then finally to all living beings. Research by Professor Barbara Fredrickson and colleagues showed that loving-kindness meditations boosted positive emotions in participants, increased their zest for life, increased their sense of purpose, whilst reducing feelings of isolation (Fredrickson et al., 2008).

In action

Given that we know humans are hardwired to be kind, I believe the following activities are less about *teaching* children to be kinder and more about giving them opportunities to be kind and to experience the kindness of others. When you try some of the following practices, be prepared to be amazed at how far the ripples of small acts of kindness can travel and how powerful those ripples can be when they sometimes turn into waves.

It's cool to be kind week

Having gotten fed up with the negative message of 'anti-bullying week' in a former school, one year I decided to rebrand it. Knowing that bullying behaviour often comes from feelings of isolation and insecurity, I wanted all the children to experience what it feels like to be kind to others and to be on the receiving end of kindness too. I wanted to create a virtuous circle of kindness, and so 'It's cool to be kind week' was born. In practice this is how it worked:

- Every child in our school, from Nursery up to Year 6, was set a home-learning challenge – to carry out a random act of kindness.

- They could choose whatever they wanted to do (from helping their grown-ups tidy the house, to baking treats for family) but they had to capture it in a photo, video or poster.

- Importantly, they had to reflect on how they felt when carrying out the act of kindness and, if possible, how the recipient felt when they received the act of kindness.

The first year was overwhelming. The whole school enthusiastically carried out their acts of kindness and the home-learning projects started flying in. The children showed their creativity in the acts of kindness that they chose to carry out. One child helped their mum do the shopping for an elderly neighbour, whilst another decided to bake cupcakes and go with their dad to the local train station to greet commuters returning from work.

There was a real buzz in our school that week, and even the staff started to carry out acts of kindness for each other by making rounds of tea and buying chocolates (no one offered to do my marking though, which was a shame). In fact, we received the dreaded Ofsted call that week and even they enjoyed it, writing in their report, 'Pupils responded particularly well to "It's Cool to be kind week"…they show great care and consideration for each other.'

Class acts of kindness

The following year, we wanted to build on the fabulous response we'd had to our first 'It's cool to be kind week'. So, as well as every child receiving the challenge of carrying out an individual random act of kindness (encouraging them to be creative and do something different to last year), we challenged every class to go out into the local community and carry out a whole class act of kindness. Maybe you could take some inspiration from some of the things the classes got up to and encourage your own class to carry out an act of kindness this school year:

- **Year 1**: Made delicious cookies in school and then went to Brockley high street to give them out to members of the public.

- **Year 2**: Were on a school trip to the Cutty Sark in Greenwich, London. They'd made a massive banner with 'Laugh more, worry less!' written on it for commuters, tourists and the general public to enjoy.

Figure 7.1: An example of a kindness note

- **Year 3**: Wrote kindness notes (see Figure 7.1) and attached them to the front of *Metro* newspapers and then handed them out to commuters at Brockley station. The school started to receive emails from people all over the London Underground network who had found a copy of the *Metro* with one of their notes, thanking the children for spreading some positivity.

- **Year 4**: Wrote beautiful inspiring quotes such as, 'To thine own self be true' and 'That smile looks good on you!' and gave them out to the public or left them on benches for people to find.

- **Year 5**: Got to Brockley station early one morning to see off commuters with renditions of 'Don't Stop Believing' by Journey. You have never seen so many commuters smiling, singing and clapping before!

- **Year 6**: Made tea and cakes so the builders working on the school extension could have a well-deserved break.

What we found was that once the week was over, the children had gotten into the habit of being kind, so acts of kindness continued to happen randomly throughout the year. The best way to continue the kindness after 'It's cool to be kind week', though, is for all of the staff to model it. Smiling at children and colleagues, holding doors open, saying 'Hello' and asking how people are, and being kind with your feedback. All of these actions will make kindness part of the 'DNA' of the school and will become infectious for the children.

Tales from the classroom

It is always so special and humbling when members of the public get in touch during 'It's cool to be kind week' to say how the children's acts of kindness have touched them. Below is just one of the many responses we have had over the years:

Dear Headteacher,

I just wanted to drop a note to say that I was moved to tears yesterday by the beautiful singing from your pupils – and staff!
It was just so heartbreakingly amazing and I will feel the warmth in my heart for a very long time to come. Gorgeous singing aside, what amazed me was the interaction between staff and students and how close and happy they all were alongside one another. As a mother of a mixed-race son it was just so beautiful to see all the students standing there together, in harmony, united. Whatever you are doing, keep doing it. If this is the future my son would have at a local primary I would be so proud and happy. Please do let the staff and students know that their show was truly inspiring.

With lots of love,
Caroline

Good deed feed

If you have any blank wall spaces in your playground or communal areas, why not liven them up with a 'good deed feed'? The idea is really simple: if children or members of staff witness someone else being kind, they can write about it on the good deed feed. This helps promote the idea that it is good to acknowledge other people's acts of kindness and to savour them. Remember, just witnessing acts of kindness can release the bonding, stress-relieving happy hormone, oxytocin!

To do this, all you need is:

- an area of wall in the playground or a display board inside the school
- laminated sheets of paper to write on, stapled to the board
- permanent marker pens to write with
- a member of staff or some responsible Year 6 pupils in charge of the pens and supervising children as they write their messages on the board.

Our school was undergoing major building works and a large section of the playground was blocked off by a plain-looking hoarding. We decided to turn the hoarding into a 'good deed feed'. At playtimes, lunchtimes and after school, children would be filling the board up (see Figure 7.2 below). Parents and carers would often be stood reading the feed before and after school. The good deed feed contained things like:

'When I was feeling sad, Shane came and made me laugh. By Shalom'

'I saw four Year 3 children helping a child in Reception who had fallen over. This made me smile. Mr Casey'

Figure 7.2: A 'good deed feed'

'I saw a man help a woman down the stairs with her buggy at the station. Kerry'

This is a simple but effective way of getting children and staff to notice all of the everyday acts of kindness that we often overlook.

Fundraising

Most primary schools I know do some kind of fundraising. But for fundraising to make a real impact on the children, it really helps if it is more engaging than simply donating £1 for wearing your own clothes on a certain day of the year. The research on prosocial spending shows that, for it to have the biggest impact on our wellbeing, we need to do the following:

1. **Make a connection**: People generally derive more happiness from spending money on people they have a connection with (Aknin et al., 2011). So when doing a fundraising project at school either choose a charity that has strong social ties to the school and local community, or choose a cause that means something to a member of the school community.

   One year, at a previous school, a member of staff had tragically lost her husband to a sudden heart attack. The following year, and with her permission, the school decided to take part in the British Heart Foundation's Three Peak Challenge. We didn't have mountains nearby to climb so we hired in a five-metre climbing wall with qualified instructors. Children learned to do rock climbing over two days and were sponsored to see how high they could climb. Parents and carers could pay to climb the wall after school. It was one of the biggest fundraisers of the year.

2. **Make an impact**: When people donate money to a cause, they don't usually get to see how the money was spent. But you get a bigger boost to your happiness levels when you know your donation has had an impact (Aknin et al., 2013b). Certain charities are very good at letting you know how they have spent your money.

   Charities like Toilet Twinning, for example, build toilet blocks in countries with poor sanitation. The idea is that schools can 'twin' their toilets with another country – i.e. if your school has four separate toilet blocks, you try to raise enough money to build four toilet blocks in your chosen country. For each toilet block you build, they send you a framed photo of the new flushing toilet block. Or, if you choose to support local charities, often their representatives will come to the school to host an assembly and show how the money has been spent. So, when choosing your charity fundraising events, make sure you can show the children the impact their donations have had.

3. **Make it fun**: If you want your children to get into the habit of giving to charities, try to make it fun! The happy hormones they will release when involved in a fun charity fundraiser will make them want to do it again and again.

I worked in a school with a high number of male staff (primary school teaching is still about 85 per cent female to 15 per cent male) and we decided to take part in Movember. This is an annual event in which men grow moustaches during November to raise awareness of men's health issues, such as prostate cancer, testicular cancer and men's suicide. Not only did the male staff look pretty foolish for a whole month (especially when doing parents' evening with a dodgy tash!) but on the last day of November, all of the children and female staff got to wear fake moustaches for the day! (see Figure 7.3)

Figure 7.3: Children wearing their fake moustaches to raise money for Movember

Befriending meditation

A type of loving-kindness practice that you could try with your class is called the 'befriending' meditation. This meditation helps children to cultivate kind and friendly feelings towards themselves and others. This is a practice inspired by *Mindfulness* by Mark Williams and Danny Penman (Williams and Penman, 2011). Ensure a strong, confident, seated posture before beginning and allow the children time to say the phrases to themselves, silently in their heads:

Start by taking three deep breaths – in through your nose and out through your mouth. Become aware of your body, sitting here, breathing. Then, with an attitude of friendliness and kindness, silently say to yourself:
'May I be healthy, may I be happy, may I be peaceful.'
Allow the phrases to sink down deep within you, as if you were dropping pebbles into a deep lake. Enjoy this feeling of showing kindness to yourself.

Then bring to mind someone you love and care for very much. Imagine them sitting in front of you smiling. Now, silently say to them:
'May you be healthy, may you be happy, may you be peaceful.'
Enjoy seeing this person looking relaxed, calm and happy.

Now bring to mind someone you know but not that well. It might be someone at school, or someone who works in a shop near where you live. You recognise them but you don't know them that well. Imagine them sitting in front of you, smiling and say to them:
'May you be healthy, may you be happy, may you be peaceful.'
Enjoy the feeling of sending kindness out to them, and seeing them happy.

Finally, bring to mind all living beings who, just like you, wish to be happy. Extend friendly, loving feelings to everyone on the planet, including yourself, saying:
'May we all be healthy, may we all be happy, may we all be peaceful.'
Enjoy this feeling of sending love and kindness out into the world.

In summary, being kind and compassionate towards others is all about connection. When we put ourselves in another's shoes and think about how our actions affect others, we are more likely to act for the benefit of others, rather than just for ourselves. The great Albert Einstein once said that to view ourselves as separate from one another and the universe was a kind of 'prison'. He went on to say that, 'Our task must be to free ourselves from this prison by widening our circle of compassion to embrace all living creatures and the whole of nature in its beauty.' (Einstein writing to Norman Salit on 4 March 1950.) Maybe teaching children the skills of kindness is one way of setting them free.

Key points

- Humans are hardwired to be kind to others. Kindness fosters social connection and cohesion, which were essential for survival in our tribal past.

- When we show kindness and compassion towards others, our bodies release happy hormones like endorphins and oxytocin, which not only make us feel happier but improve our health too.

- A virtuous circle can begin, as being kind makes us happier and when we're happier, we're more likely to be kind.

- Schools can host 'kindness weeks' in which children are encouraged to carry out random acts of kindness. Even whole classes can go out into the local community to carry out class acts of kindness.

- Get children to notice everyday acts of kindness by creating a 'good deed feed' in your school.

- When fundraising in school, ensure children make a connection with the good cause, allow them to see the impact their fundraising has and make it fun for them!

- Children can cultivate kind feelings towards themselves and others by trying a 'befriending' meditation.

Chapter 8
How our thoughts shape our world

Teaching is the greatest act of optimism.

– Colleen Wilcox

Chapter overview

In this chapter, we'll look at why it pays to be more optimistic, in terms of health and happiness. We'll understand how children's mental chatter affects their levels of optimism, and look at what we can do to nudge our pupils to look on the brighter side of life.

In theory	In action
• Optimism and its benefits	• Thoughts for the day
• Explanatory style	• Influencing explanatory style
• ABC model	• Conscience alley
• Reframing	• Music
• Priming	• Nature

In theory

Optimism and its benefits

Everyone knows the old saying that an optimist sees a half-drunk glass as being 'half-full', whereas a pessimist sees it as being 'half-empty'. But what's the big deal? Why does it matter that we all see the world differently? Well, increasing evidence shows that being more optimistic can have a wide range of positive implications for our happiness and well-being. For example, studies have shown that optimistic people tend to:

1. report higher levels of subjective wellbeing and happiness (Ferguson and Goodwin, 2010)

2. show higher levels of positive emotion (Chang and Sanna, 2001)

3. have better overall health and are less prone to disease (Seligman, 2011)

4. have less chance of suffering from clinical depression (Kahneman, 2011).

Psychologists describe optimism as the expectation that the future will be socially desirable, good and pleasurable and, although genetics and upbringing play a large part in affecting our levels of optimism, it is still a skill we can learn. Moreover, Martin Seligman believes it is a skill that could be taught in schools as an antidote to depression, a way of increasing life satisfaction, and an aid to better learning and creativity (Seligman et al., 2009).

Blind optimism vs. realistic optimism

Although it is clear that having a more optimistic outlook is beneficial to us, it is important to note that there are downsides to being overly optimistic as well. Studies show that people who are *too* optimistic:

1. are often unable to delay gratification and so want everything immediately

2. have difficulty sizing up situations realistically and ignore important pitfalls

3. can make unwise decisions (e.g. making highly risky investments) (Davidson and Begley, 2012, p. 227)

4. can suffer from 'false-hope syndrome', where they stick with ridiculous expectations way past the point when they should have given up or changed tactics (Dolan, 2015, p. 97).

This is often known as 'blind optimism', where people continue to feel the future will turn out brilliantly, despite glaringly obvious obstacles or problems. Instead, positive psychologists argue it is better to be aiming for 'realistic optimism'. According to Paul Dolan, this is where 'We should expect the best but have a contingency plan for the worst.' (Dolan, 2015,

p. 97) Realistic optimism is also where you don't filter out the risks involved in a given situation, but you do filter out unhelpful negative thoughts that might be holding you back.

Explanatory style

Where we fall on the spectrum of optimism and pessimism is largely affected by our 'explanatory style', which is the mental conversations or chatter we have with ourselves when good and bad things happen to and around us. When something happens to us, we can explain it as being temporary (a one-off) or permanent (it will last forever), local (specific to that situation) or global (it affects other areas of our lives too), and personal (we are the cause of the event) or impersonal (the event has nothing to do with us).

The table below shows the explanatory styles of an optimist and a pessimist, in response to a *negative* event:

Optimist	Pessimist
Temporary: 'This isn't what I had planned, but it won't last forever.'	**Permanent:** 'It is always going to be like this, no matter what I try.'
Local: 'This isn't great but at least other things in my life are going well.'	**Global:** 'This means everything is ruined now.'
Impersonal: 'I tried my best, but this was out of my control.'	**Personal:** 'This is all my fault.'

But look what happens to the explanatory styles of an optimist and pessimist in response to a *positive* event:

Optimist	Pessimist
Permanent: 'If I keep doing what I'm doing, I can expect positive outcomes like this.'	**Temporary:** 'This won't last forever.'
Global: 'This will positively affect other areas of my life too.'	**Local:** 'Just because this went well doesn't mean anything else will.'
Personal: 'I worked hard and made this happen.'	**Impersonal:** 'I got lucky; this didn't have much to do with me.'

The way optimists and pessimists view events, both good and bad, are completely opposite to each other. Whereas optimists can take credit for good events happening, and see them positively affecting other areas of their lives, pessimists see these as flukes and that life will go back to being rubbish as normal.

According to Seligman, two of the main ways we develop our explanatory styles in childhood are by:

1. **Imitating our parents**: How our parents, especially our mothers, explain good and bad events to us, directly impacts our own explanatory style. We will imitate the optimism or pessimism of our parents.

2. **Adult feedback or criticism**: When we are praised or scolded by adults, we internalise the messages. For example, if a parent or teacher tells us, 'You *never* listen properly!' we may believe that, in any given situation, we find it hard to listen to what's going on. In turn this affects our behaviour, so we're more likely to switch off because we believe we lack the ability to pay attention (Seligman, 2002).

This shows how important teachers are in helping shape children's explanatory styles. By giving your pupils a realistic and optimistic example to imitate and by choosing your words carefully when feeding back to them, you can help positively influence their explanatory style. We'll look at how we can do this in more detail in the 'in action' section (p. 134).

ABC model

The good news is, our explanatory styles and levels of optimism can be trained just like any other skill. Positive psychologist, Ed Diener, explains that we can teach people to get better at 'recognising unhelpful thinking strategies and replacing them with positive ones.' (Diener and Biswas-Diener, 2008, p. 193) One way to do this is to teach the ABC model derived from the work of psychologist Albert Ellis (Ellis, 1962). The A stands for an adversity; B stands for your beliefs about the event; and C stands for your consequent feelings and actions (see Figure 8.1). One of the main ideas behind the ABC model is that our emotions do not follow inevitably from external events but, rather, from our *beliefs*

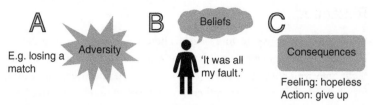

Figure 8.1: The ABC model illustrated

and *thoughts* about those events. A major insight is that we can actually exercise some *choice* over what we think about an event. The aim is to not let unhelpful and negative thinking run away with itself unchecked (remember from Chapter 3, p. 45 how strong our negativity bias can be?), but instead, to challenge these thoughts and be more flexible and accurate with our thinking, which in turn changes what we feel and how we behave.

For example, imagine you're about to teach a lesson which is to be observed by a senior member of staff (A – an adversity). You start to worry that the lesson won't go so well and that you will get poor feedback (B – your beliefs). You end up feeling anxious and stressed and this may lead to you teaching a poor-quality lesson (C – consequences). Because we have some choice over our thoughts and beliefs, we can challenge the thought that the lesson won't go well. We could bring to mind numerous other times when we've been observed and had positive feedback. We could simply notice the thought and let it go (using our mindfulness practice from Chapter 2, p. 27) and take some deep, calming breaths. Or we could remind ourselves that the person observing us is an amenable colleague and will give fair and honest feedback that we can learn from. Rather than letting an unhelpful and negative thought escalate and start to deplete us, we catch it early, challenge it and choose a more helpful response.

The ability to choose one's response to any given situation is perfectly embodied by Victor Frankl in his book, *Man's Search For Meaning*. Frankl, a Jewish psychiatrist, was incarcerated in Auschwitz concentration camp during the Second World War but was one of the few that survived. In his book, he writes these powerful words, 'Everything can be taken from a man but one thing: the last of human freedoms – to choose one's attitude in any given set of circumstances.' (Frankl, 1946)

Reframing

Shakespeare once wrote in *Hamlet*, 'There is nothing either good or bad, but thinking makes it so.' It turns out that this underlies another technique we could use when faced with challenging situations which is called 'reframing'. This is a process where we 'reframe' a negative situation into a positive one by changing our perspective. So, the 'problem' of the impending lesson observation becomes the 'opportunity' to show how much our teaching practice has improved. Or your 'weakness' of spending too much money on others at Christmas is viewed as your 'strength' of being generous and kind. Reframing is about acknowledging that there is always a different perspective to view 'negative' events from. As the Dalai Lama writes in *The Art of Happiness*, 'One must realise that every phenomena, every event, has different aspects. Everything is of a relative nature.' (His Holiness, the Dalai Lama and Cutler, 1999, p. 173)

Harvard Business School psychologist, Alison Wood, has carried out a number of experiments to look at a type of reframing she calls 'anxiety reappraisal'. In one study, Wood asked her participants to do various scary things from public speaking to sitting a maths exam. She found that when the participants reframed their nerves as 'excitement' rather than 'anxiety', their performance improved (Brooks, 2014). Teachers can employ this technique to help manage their pupils' levels of anxiety and stress, as well as their own. As we learned in Chapter 5 (p. 77), just the right level of arousal and stress in the classroom leads to the greatest performance.

Priming

Psychologists have discovered that we can influence people to think and behave in certain desirable ways and this is known as 'priming'. For example, experiments have shown that using a citrus air freshener makes it far more likely that people will clear up after themselves and that medical students will comply with hand hygiene regulations (Dolan, 2015, p. 127). The smell of citrus in the air mentally prepares the mind (on a completely subconscious level) for cleanliness, and so people think and behave in more hygienic ways. Something to bear in mind for the school toilets!

It transpires that, through priming, we can nudge people to feel more optimistic, hopeful, and even kinder towards others. University of California psychologists, Philip Shaver and Mario Mikulincer, were looking for ways to shift people who were insecurely attached to feeling more secure. By showing people words like 'love', or having them recall happy memories of being with loved ones, they were able to induce that shift, at least temporarily. Shaver explains, 'Attachment words trigger a kind of comfort that makes tolerance for others more available mentally, even in insecure people, whose natural inclination is intolerance and lack of compassion.' (Shaver in Goleman, 2015, p. 35)

Schools are often filled with quotes and aphorisms to try and motivate their pupils, which is another form of priming. One thing to bear in mind is that we tend to be drawn to aphorisms that rhyme and roll off the tongue nicely. A study by cognitive scientists found that pithy sayings that rhymed were found to be more believable by participants than sayings that had the same meaning but didn't rhyme (McGlone and Tofighbakhsh, 2000). For example, we would believe the 'truth' of Napoleon Hill's statement 'Whatever the mind of man can conceive and believe, it can achieve' more than if it was changed to, 'Whatever the mind of man can conceive and believe, it can do.' Therefore, the words, posters, phrases and messages that appear around schools are important. They are mentally priming your pupils and staff, affecting how they think and behave.

Other primes to consider for schools are children's and staff members' exposure to nature and music. Numerous studies show the amazing wellbeing benefits of immersing people in natural surroundings. One experiment in Japan involved participants walking in either a forest or an urban area. Results showed that the forest walkers had lower heart rates, improved mood and lower levels of stress and anxiety than the urban walkers (Lee et al., 2014). But, if you do not have a forest nearby, have no fear; simply looking at nature can positively affect wellbeing. Hospital patients recovering from surgery were shown in one study to recover more quickly if their bed looked out on views of nature, rather than on views of a brick wall (Ulrich, 1984). Simply having plants in a room can lower levels of stress (Dolan, 2015, p. 128) and, as we saw in Chapter 7 (pp. 114–15), you'll really boost wellbeing if you actively take care of the plants yourself. Similarly, playing music can boost our mood and levels of optimism. Dolan explains, 'It most strongly affects the brain region associated with positive emotion and memory in a way that no other input to our happiness production process can.' (Dolan, 2015, p. 150)

In action

Teachers can be hugely influential in their pupils' lives. It is very common for children to go home and challenge their parents based on what their teachers have said at school. When children say to their parents, 'Well, actually, Miss Davis said that…' or, 'Mr Bond says that…' it shows that our pupils are actually listening to what we are saying and, more importantly, we are having an effect on what they think and how they behave. With this great power comes great responsibility! The following ideas will guide you in helping shape your pupils' thoughts so they feel inspired and empowered.

Thoughts for the day

To mentally prime your pupils to think more optimistically, you could start your morning with a 'thought for the day'. These are simply thoughts, sayings, quotes or aphorisms to get your children thinking and maybe to provoke a positive emotional response. The charity, Action for Happiness, regularly post beautifully-illustrated quotes on social media and I often use these in my class. Here is how you could do it too:

- Choose an inspiring quote or saying to display on your board (see Figure 8.2 for an example). You could use the 'Inspiring words' Pinterest board by Action for Happiness for inspiration (**www. pinterest.co.uk/actionhappiness/inspiring-words**).

- As the children come into class, ask them to silently read the 'thought for the day' to themselves and think about what it means.

- After all of the children have had a chance to read and digest the thought, ask a child to read it out loud and host a short discussion about what it could mean.

- You could then print the poster off and add it to a 'thoughts for the day' board (see Figure 8.3 as an example). You can download a free 'thought for the day' display banner here: **www.teachappy.co.uk/resources-and-downloads**.

Figure 8.2: A 'thought for the day' poster (credit: Julia_Henze, iStockphoto)

A lovely thing that grew out of the 'thought for the day' in my class was that during the register one morning, when I said, 'Good morning, Andy,' rather than replying, 'Good morning, Mr Bethune,' as had happened every other day up until then, Andy decided to reply with a thought for the day. 'One kind word can change someone's entire day, Mr Bethune,' came Andy's reply. I smiled, the other children giggled and it started a new way of replying during the register. 'Just be nice, Mr Bethune.' 'A good laugh recharges your batteries, Mr Bethune.' 'If plan A doesn't work, there are 25 other letters in the alphabet. Stay cool, Mr Bethune.' Now, instead of saying a thought for the day back to me, they pass it on to the next person on the register. Some children have even started to make up their own thoughts for the day or have said ones they have read outside of school. In terms of starting your day on a positive and optimistic note, it doesn't get much better than this!

Figure 8.3: 'Thoughts for the day' display

I hasten to add, this is not about brainwashing children to believe certain things, which is why discussion is a key part of this idea. Children are free to debate and challenge the thought for the day. I would also recommend that you are quite selective with the thoughts you choose. Lots of quotes and sayings around happiness can be unhelpful and problematic. For example, a saying like, 'If it doesn't make you happy, don't do it' is complete nonsense, as there are many important and meaningful things that might not bring immediate positive emotions (like working hard on a difficult project or looking after a friend who is upset). However, as your children get more familiar with discussing the thoughts for the day, and their thinking becomes more creative and flexible, you could choose to put a more controversial thought up like, 'Always be happy', and see what they think about it. My bet is, they'll easily find the flaws in sayings like these.

Tales from the classroom

Angela was stood at the top of the 50-metre-long zip wire and she had frozen. Team Year 4 Green had gone to an outdoor activity park as an end of term treat. Angela was having fun up until this point but now her nerves had gotten the better of her. Her teammates gathered round the bottom of the tall tree that she was stood upon and they were calling her name to cheer her on. It just made things worse, now that an audience was there to watch her clinging to the trunk. But then her friend Sofia called out.

'Angela! Listen to me! If you believe you can, or you believe you can't, you're right!' Sofia shouted.

She had just quoted Henry Ford, one of our previous thoughts for the day. Sofia continued, 'I believe you can, Angela! You can do this!'

Spurred on by her friend and her insightful words, Angela edged closer to the zip wire and then…

'AAAAAAAAAAAAAHHHHHHHHHHHHHHH!' came the scream from one of the most diminutive, but now one of the bravest, children you have ever seen.

A few seconds later, Angela was back on solid earth. Cheers from her classmates echoed throughout the forest and Sofia ran over to hug her friend.

Influencing explanatory style

The children in your class will have a whole range of explanatory styles, but there is a lot you can do as their teacher to influence them to be more optimistic. Many of the ideas we have explored in the book already are designed to prime your children to think optimistically about certain things:

- **Tribal classroom**: Signals to children that they matter, they are part of something bigger than themselves, and that people care about them (Chapter 1, p. 11).

- **Mindfulness**: Teaches children that their thoughts aren't facts and they don't have to believe them. They can choose to let them go and take their attention elsewhere (Chapter 2, p. 27).

- **What went well**: Helps children realise there is always something to be grateful for and to appreciate, and that the little things matter (Chapter 3, p. 45).

- **Neuroplasticity**: Lets children know they have the capacity and potential to learn new things and master new skills (Chapter 4, p. 61).

- **Stretch zone**: Shows children that hard work is necessary to improve, mistakes can be good, that they learn the most when they are challenged and that feeling a bit nervous when stretching yourself is normal (Chapter 5, p. 77).

- **Flow and strengths**: Teaches children that hard work can be fun, that challenging themselves can make them feel good and that we all have strengths we can grow (Chapter 6, p. 93).

- **It's cool to be kind**: Allows children to experience the joy of giving and receiving kindness. It shows them that there is goodness in the world and that they have the power to spread that goodness themselves (Chapter 7, p. 111).

It is also helpful to be mindful about the praise and feedback we give, as the children will internalise it and it will become part of their explanatory style. This requires teachers being aware of their own explanatory styles and where they fall on the optimism and pessimism scale. So, when giving feedback to children consider the following:

- **Keep it positive**: A ratio of five positive comments to every negative one is found in most positive relationships (Gottman, 1994). As we saw in Chapter 1 (p. 16), the ratio may need to be higher when working with children.

- **Model an optimistic explanatory style**: When things go wrong in class, or you deal with challenging behaviour, explain it to pupils in a way that shows it's temporary ('It won't be like this forever'), local ('This has gone wrong here but other areas are going well') and impersonal ('That was a bad choice but you are not a bad person').

- **Challenge and reframe**: When pupils show pessimistic and inaccurate thinking in class, don't let the thoughts go unchallenged. For example, if Jennifer is struggling on a maths problem and says, 'I'm rubbish at maths!', you could ask if that statement is *always* true. You could help her recall lessons and areas of maths that she has succeeded at. You could reframe the situation by telling her that if she's struggling, that means the work is challenging and so she's working in the stretch zone and her brain is growing lots by working on this tricky problem.

Conscience alley

A fun and interactive way to get the children to reflect on explanatory styles (you could describe these to your class as the conversations or chatter we all have in our heads when good and bad things happen) is to use a drama activity called 'conscience alley'. Here is how it could work:

- Get the children to generate a list of negative scenarios that they might experience in their lives (e.g. getting a low score on a test, losing a sports match, falling out with a friend).

- Explain that when we experience these negative events, we can often have negative thoughts about what has just happened. Sometimes these thoughts *exaggerate* how bad the situation is.

- Select a scenario to explore (e.g. losing a football match) and choose one child to walk down the conscience alley. The other children form two equal lines standing opposite each other, creating the alleyway for the first child to walk down.

- Now, as the first child takes one step forward, each child in the alley takes it in turns to say out loud a *negative* thought that they might be having. 'I'm rubbish at football!', 'No one wants me on their team!', 'My team is so bad!' or 'My team will never win anything!'

- Get the children to reflect on the feelings they might experience if those are the thoughts they're having when something goes wrong in their life. What might the person be feeling when having these thoughts? How might they behave as a result? Were the thoughts kind? Were they accurate? Are they likely to help the person deal with the problem?

- Do the activity again but, this time, ask the children to *reframe* the situation and choose more *realistically optimistic* thoughts as their classmate walks down conscience alley. 'Never mind, it wasn't my fault.' 'I can work on my mistakes in training.' 'We played our best, the other team were just better today.' 'It still felt good to run around and play footy with my friends!'

- Ask the children to reflect again. How did these thoughts affect what the person might be feeling? Were the thoughts kinder? Were they more accurate? Are they more likely to help the person deal with the problem?

- It might be helpful to end by showing the ABC model image (Figure 8.1, p. 131) and explaining that in any situation we have the power to choose what thoughts we have, which in turn affects what we may feel and how we might behave. If our thoughts are particularly negative, we can practise swapping them with more positive ones.

Music

It may be because I worked in the music industry for several years before retraining to become a teacher, but I play a lot of music in my classroom. I love to start my day with music, especially when setting up my classroom, but I also like to play it during the day, when the children enter the classroom in the morning, for example, or during some lessons. Why not experiment with the following ideas?

- Play an uplifting piece of music when your class come in first thing in the morning. I love *The Lark Ascending* by Ralph Vaughan Williams.

- Have your 'thought of the day' on the board whilst the music is playing, so children have something to contemplate as they sit down.

- Have calm and peaceful music playing in the communal areas of your school like the reception area and hall.

- During lessons when you want to encourage 'silent' working (or at least no talking), play some classical or instrumental music in the background to enable them to focus better. (Avoid having the music on too loud, or it becoming a distraction to pupils.)

- Intersperse your day with music. Share with your class some of your favourite tracks and music videos at the end of the day. Expose them to styles and genres they might not have heard before. (Be sure to check lyric and video content is age-appropriate!)

- Get your children moving to music. It's instinctive to want to move your body when you hear a good beat and rhythm, so use music to get your class out of their seats. (See pp. 156–7 for ideas on incorporating dance into your lessons.)

Nature

Some schools are lucky with the amount of green space and natural surroundings they have. My current school has a large grass playing field, a Japanese sensory garden and a 'wild wood' where our forest school takes place. But, previously, I worked in an inner-London primary school with not a patch of grass in sight. But that didn't mean we were lacking in nature. A very green-fingered teaching assistant called Helen became the school gardener and planted wherever she could. The playground was abloom with trees, plants, flowers and shrubs and it looked stunning! The school also had helpful parents who ran an allotment club after school, where children planted and grew fruit and vegetables. So, whether your school has acres of grassland or is a concrete jungle, try to get as much nature as possible in your school using these ideas:

- If your school has an eco-team, task them with getting more plants, shrubs and flowers in and around your school. If your school doesn't have an eco-team, go to **www.eco-schools.org.uk** to learn more and then set one up.

- Approach parents, local flower shops and garden nurseries to see if they will donate any plants to your school.

- Have lots of low-maintenance plants in classrooms and communal areas around the school. Elect pupils to be plant monitors on rotation to care for the plants.

- Set up an outside area as a dedicated 'allotment'. Grow seasonal fruit and vegetables and give the children opportunities to plant, pick and eat the produce!
- If your school has lots of green space, see if you can set up a forest school. Go to **www.forestschoolassociation.org** to find out more.

Key points

- Having a realistic optimistic outlook on life has many health and wellbeing benefits.
- Our levels of optimism are heavily influenced by our explanatory styles, which are shaped by our parents and the feedback and criticism we receive and internalise.
- We can become more optimistic by changing how we think about the good and bad events in our lives. Our thoughts and beliefs are also 'primed' by the things we read and by our environment.
- Start your day in class with a positive thought for the day. Get the children to discuss what it means and how it relates to happiness.
- Positively influence your pupils' explanatory styles by setting a good example and by helping them to challenge and reframe their inaccurate negative beliefs.
- Use the drama activity 'conscience alley' to explore how optimistic and pessimistic thinking can affect what we feel and how we behave. Get children to practise 'reframing' negative situations into positive ones.
- Play more music during the day. It can lift mood, get children moving and help them to concentrate.
- Fill your class with nature. Plants have a calming effect on pupils and the effect is even greater if pupils are tasked with caring for them.

Chapter 9
Exercise makes me happy

If you are in a bad mood, go for a walk. If you are still in a bad mood, go for another walk.

– Hippocrates

Chapter overview

In this chapter, we'll discover why exercise might be one of the most underrated ways in which we can improve our happiness and wellbeing. We'll look at exactly what happens in our children's brains and bodies when they get moving and how we can incorporate more exercise into the school day.

In theory	In action
• The problem	• The Daily Mile
• Exercise as medicine	• Hindu squats
• Dosage	• Go Noodle
	• Yoga
	• Dance

In theory

The problem

There is a growing epidemic in the UK and it is the increasing inactivity of our children. According to government statistics, nearly a third of children aged two to 15 are obese and younger generations are becoming obese at earlier ages and staying obese for longer (UK Government, 2017). The government has set out to tackle this by introducing a 'sugar tax' on fizzy drinks and increasing the sports funding that primary schools receive. Although increasing obesity levels are an obvious sign that our children are exercising less, the fact is that inactivity is bad for you whether you're overweight or stick thin. In his book, *Flourish*, Martin Seligman shares evidence from one study that showed that 'the fit, but fat, individual has almost half the risk of death of the unfit, fat individual.' Other data he explores shows that if you are unfit, 'normal and obese people both have a high risk for death, and it does not seem to matter if you are fat or thin.' (Seligman, 2011, pp. 216–7)

We should be quite worried that low fitness has such poor health outcomes because very few of our children are as active as they could be. The Chief Medical Officer in the UK says that children between the ages of five and 18 should be taking part in *at least* 60 minutes of moderate to vigorous activity *every day* (UK Government, 2011). However, a report published by the British Heart Foundation National Centre for Physical Activity and Health showed that, in England, 84 per cent of girls and 79 per cent of boys aged five to 15 do *not* meet these physical activity guidelines (Townsend et al., 2015). This is shocking! But it really isn't surprising when you consider that a report commissioned by the Youth Sport Trust in 2015 showed that primary schools are spending about 20 per cent less time on PE in Key Stage 1 and about ten per cent less time in Key Stage 2 (comparing data from 2009/10 to 2013/14). (Youth Sport Trust, 2015) To add insult to injury, have a guess where children spend a disproportionate amount of time sitting down and being sedentary? That's right, at schools! This is a big problem because sedentary behaviour has been linked in adulthood to increased chances of heart disease, diabetes, some types of cancer and depression. (Biddle et al., 2010) In short, schools need to do more to get their children out of their seats and moving.

Exercise as medicine

According to Public Health England, the direct cost of obesity to the NHS is estimated to be over six billion pounds a year (Public Health England, 2017). But there is a medicine that schools can administer to its children not only to prevent the rise of obesity, but also to help reverse its negative effects. This medicine costs nothing to give out, it starts working immediately, it is easy and fun to take and one of its side effects is chronic smiling and happiness. This medicine is exercise! Let's have a look at how this medicine can positively affect our body and mind.

Health

Not only does exercise promote stronger muscles and bones, but it boosts the immune system too, meaning you'll get ill less and recover more quickly from illnesses if you're fit. According to the NHS, regular exercise also reduces your risk of major illnesses such as heart disease, stroke, type 2 diabetes and cancer by up to 50 per cent, as well as lowering your risk of early death by up to 30 per cent (NHS Choices, 2015). Whereas sitting down for prolonged periods of time is linked with shortening your lifespan, conversely, there is compelling evidence that the more physically fit you are, the longer you can expect to live (King, 2016, p. 79).

Happiness

Exercise can have profound positive effects on our moods. When we do strenuous physical activity, our bodies release endorphins. Endorphins are nature's way of dulling pain (in case we are fighting or running away from a lion on the savannah) and calming the mind, so we can focus on the task in hand. In his book, *Spark!*, John Ratey explains that endorphins work like the powerful painkiller morphine and 'produce euphoria in the mind'. (Ratey and Hagerman, 2010, p. 117) This is why people often report a 'runner's high' after completing a marathon. But, we don't have to run 26.2 miles to get this high (even just thinking about it makes me tired). Studies also show simply going for a walk can lift our mood. Psychologist Paul Taylor says that, 'Walking works like a drug, and it starts working even after a few steps.' (Montgomery, 2015, p. 188)

Regular exercise also boosts our body image and self-esteem. People who take part in regular exercise feel better about themselves generally. Vanessa King believes this is important because: 'Poor body image and low self-esteem, experienced by both men and women, is linked with depression, anxiety and with the likelihood of detrimental health behaviours such as smoking, excessive alcohol consumption and extreme dieting.' (King, 2016, p. 83)

Overall, regular exercise appears to make children feel better about their lives. The report by PISA on student wellbeing (OECD, 2017) showed that active children are not only less likely to skip school, feel anxious about schoolwork or be bullied, but the report goes on to state that, 'Physically active students report higher levels of life satisfaction…and psychological wellbeing.' Life appears to feel better when we get moving.

Stress, anxiety and depression

As we have read in earlier chapters, when we perceive a threat, our amygdala kicks in, and our bodies prepare for fight or flight. Stress hormones like adrenaline and cortisol flood our body, giving us extra energy, so we can defend ourselves or run away. The problem in this day and age is, rather than escaping or fighting, we sit there getting more stressed, worried and anxious, not knowing what to do. But we are meant to move when the stress response kicks in! John Ratey explains that, 'When we exercise in response to stress, we're doing what human beings have evolved to do over the past several million years.' (Ratey and Hagerman, 2010, p. 64) By moving our bodies after stressful events, we actually use up all of the biochemicals and extra energy that have flooded our system (which can cause us harm if left unattended). It is no surprise then that people who are more physically active report fewer incidences of emotional distress and feelings of anxiousness, as well as reacting less when things go awry and recovering more quickly when they do (King, 2016, pp. 83–4). Exercise, therefore, helps boost our levels of resilience by allowing us to manage our levels of stress and anxiety.

There is even evidence that shows that exercise can help people suffering from clinical depression. One study split participants suffering with depression into three groups to try out different interventions. The first group were given antidepressants, the second group had to exercise for 45 minutes three times a week, and the third group did a combination of the two (Babyak et al., 2000). After four months, all three groups experienced similar improvements in their happiness levels proving that exercise can be as effective as the most potent antidepressants. But, the most remarkable finding from the study came six months later when the participants were assessed to see who had relapsed into depression. Of the medication group, 38 per cent had relapsed into depression. The combination group fared slightly better, with 31 per cent suffering a relapse. Astonishingly, the exercise group's relapse rate was only nine per cent! So, not only is exercise a fast-working medicine at lifting your mood, it appears to be a long-lasting one too.

The brain

If you think of your brain like a plant, then exercise produces a fertiliser to help your brain grow. There is something our brains produce called brain-derived neurotrophic factor (BDNF) which helps build and maintain the brain circuitry. Ratey explains that BDNF 'improves the functions of neurons, encourages their growth, and strengthens and protects them against the natural process of cell death.' (Ratey and Hagerman, 2010, p. 40) He describes BDNF as Miracle-Gro® for the brain. It turns out that when we exercise, our bodies produce more BDNF, which means that exercise directly helps our brains grow new neurons and protect the ones that are already there. This may explain why physically active adults are less likely to experience dementia or Alzheimer's in later life (King, 2016, p. 85). Furthermore, in a 2007 study that Ratey cites, researchers found that when learning new vocabulary, participants learned them 20 per cent faster after they did some exercise and that the rate of learning correlated with the increased levels of BDNF (King, 2016, p. 45).

It seems that exercise perfectly primes the brain for learning. Straight after exercise, with our heart rates increased, our heart pumps more blood, oxygen and glucose up to our brains. This wakes our brains up, helps them be alert to new information and be able to pay attention. The happy hormones that are released after exercise, like endorphins and dopamine, put us in a good mood, help us be more creative and flexible in our thinking, and motivate us to want to learn. Numerous studies show that fitter children tend to perform better academically. A 2013 report by the American Institute of Medicine stated that fitter children 'show greater attention, have faster cognitive processing speed and perform better on standardized academic tests than children who are less active.' (Institute of Medicine, 2013) Ratey explains that when children's brain activity is measured, there is 'more activity in fit kids' brains, indicating that more neurons involved in attention were being recruited for a given task.' (Ratey and Hagerman, 2010, p. 25)

Dosage

So, if exercise is the medicine, what dosage do we need to take in order to gain from all of the benefits listed above? Let's look at some various forms of exercise:

Walking

In his brilliant visual lecture called '23 and ½ hours' (**ed.ted.com/featured/Mot8KdLT**), Dr Mike Evans makes the case that we can benefit hugely from spending 30 minutes a day walking, and limiting our sitting and sleeping to the remaining 23 and a half hours in the day. It's an excellent and compelling video and reassuring that all we need to do is go for a brisk walk!

Running

When Elaine Wyllie was headteacher of St. Ninians Primary School in Scotland, she became concerned when the school's sports coach told her the children were shattered after the warm-ups in PE lessons. They were simply unfit. She decided to do something about it and created the 'Daily Mile' where the children had to jog or run for 15 minutes every day (children can roughly cover a mile in this amount of time). Due to the success of the scheme at Elaine's school where obesity levels at the school are shown to be about 45 per cent less than the national average (The Daily Mile, 2018), the Daily Mile has been rolled out nationally.

In 2016, a study was conducted at Coppermill Primary School in London to evaluate the impact of the Daily Mile (London Playing Fields Foundation, 2016). Two Year 5 and one Year 6 class took part in the Daily Mile three times a week, over an eight-week period. Not only did pupils register big improvements in fitness levels, they showed increases in self-esteem, and the Year 6 class, who also completed the Daily Mile every morning before sitting their SATs exams, scored significantly higher than the national average on their reading, writing, grammar and maths tests. See more about how you can incorporate the Daily Mile into your school routine in the 'In action' section (p. 150).

Yoga and dance

What Works Centre for Wellbeing (2017) carried out a large review of published reports on sport and wellbeing, called *Sport, Dance and Young People*. The review found that yoga-type activities 'can improve feelings of anxiety, depression, anger, attention and overall subjective wellbeing'. Yoga is also a great way to experience flow, so much so, that Csikszentmihalyi notes, 'it makes sense to think of yoga as a very thoroughly planned flow activity.' (Csikszentmihalyi, 2002, p. 105) It seems that yoga is a really good workout for the body and the mind.

Similarly, the review also showed that taking part in aerobic and hip-hop dance can boost our mood, and dance training is shown to be effective in lowering self-reported depression (What Works Centre for Wellbeing, 2017). Ratey also believes learning irregular rhythms and dance patterns can help improve brain plasticity (Ratey and Hagerman, 2010, p. 56).

See more on how to use yoga and dance in your class in the 'In action' section (p. 155).

Group movement

If we can combine physical activity with helping children feel part of a team (or tribe!) then that can be really positive for their wellbeing. The *Sport, Dance and Young People* review cited above demonstrated that, 'On average, across all activities including sport, those who were alone demonstrated lower happiness, higher anxiety and lower sense of purpose.' (What Works Centre for Wellbeing, 2017) Chapter 1 of this book has already illustrated the power of feeling part of a team (p. 11), so it's no surprise that when we take part in sports as a group or team, we tend to be happier. The review also confirmed that playing sports outdoors is better for young people's wellbeing than playing inside, so get outside in nature whenever you can.

In action

The key thing to remember with this chapter is that it is all about *movement*. We need to get our children sitting down less and moving more and the following activities will allow you to do this in a way that not only supports their learning but also develops long-term healthy habits.

The Daily Mile

One of the best things about introducing the Daily Mile into your school is that it costs absolutely no money! It also only takes 15 minutes out of your day. As a result of the Daily Mile, your class are more likely to be alert in lessons, feel better about themselves, and be fitter and healthier too. Here are some of the key things to bear in mind to get your children running the Daily Mile:

- **Keep it simple**: Do not overcomplicate what is a very straightforward intervention. The children simply need to have a safe, open space to be able to run laps for 15 minutes.

- **Start off small**: We introduced the Daily Mile incrementally at my school. The children ran for five minutes daily in the first week, then ten minutes in the second, and then built up to 15 minutes by the third week.

- **Make it fun**: Allow the children to talk and chat as they run around, as this is as much a social exercise as it is a fitness one.

- **Join in**: Teachers and teaching assistants can join in too. I love running with the children. Not only do I benefit from the fresh air and endorphins, but I get to chat to my class and check in with my more vulnerable pupils in an informal way.

- **Make it inclusive**: The Daily Mile is not a competition or a race. Everyone is encouraged to jog or run for the full 15 minutes at his or her own pace. If children have mobility issues, adapt to suit their needs.

- **Go with the flow**: It's best if the Daily Mile is fitted into your timetable in a flexible way. My class normally complete it at the same time every morning but, if weather or changes to the timetable mean we can't, we'll fit it in elsewhere that day.

- **Do it daily**: Unless it is really tipping it down, or there are gale-force winds, get outside. At a minimum, complete the Daily Mile three times a week. The Daily Mile is also meant to be in *addition* to your weekly PE lessons (not as a warm-up for PE).

- **Don't change kit**: Children can run the mile in their normal uniform. Ensure children have appropriate footwear to run in (a quick change into trainers works or make black trainers part of your school uniform).

- **For more information**: Go to **www.thedailymile.co.uk/ getting-started**.

My school has been doing the Daily Mile for over a year now and the children really love taking part (see Figure 9.1). If you ever forget to do it, your class will be sure to remind you!

To help keep the children at my school engaged with the Daily Mile, we have used the following ways to keep it fresh and interesting:

- In our weekly wellbeing assembly, using an interactive online map (**www.freemaptools.com/radius-around-point.htm**), we worked out how far our children had run around the world. If every child in every class from Year 1 to Year 6 ran a mile, that would be 180 miles a day, or 900 miles in a week (which was enough to reach Berlin, but not quite far enough to make it to Barcelona!). The children really enjoyed seeing how far they had collectively travelled around the globe each week.

Figure 9.1: Team Nevelson running the Daily Mile

- We have introduced Daily Mile marathon wristbands. For every 26 Daily Miles the children complete (which should take just over a half term), they'll receive a rubber wristband.

- To encourage older residents to keep physically active, Hertfordshire Council are asking their Daily Mile schools to invite the children's grandparents in to complete the mile with them. With the council's help, my school will host a Daily Mile grandparent morning. If successful, it could become an annual event.

- Our school became the proud owners of a school dog, Milo. Milo will often join classes on their mile run and he is probably the best motivator we've seen for getting the children moving.

Tales from the classroom

The first year we introduced the 'long-distance' race into our annual sports day was a bit of a disaster. A particularly hot day didn't help matters, but a few of the children either didn't have the stamina to complete the race or crossed the line crying. The children weren't fit enough for it. We were determined to improve the children's experience of the long-distance race by next year.

In the preceding gap, the children had been introduced to the Daily Mile. They completed it on most days, in rain or shine. Their fitness levels increased, they enjoyed chatting to their friends as they ran, and it was nice just to be outside and moving.

Fast-forward a year, and it was sports day again. As PE coordinator, I had decided along with our sports coach, Mr Jones, to *increase* the length of the long-distance race. We practised the longer distance in our PE lessons leading up to sports day and coached the children in how to pace themselves. Crucially, we made it clear to the children that the long-distance race was *shorter* than one mile, so we knew everyone could complete it.

On the day, the children did not let us down. Everyone completed the long-distance race, no one gave up and there were no tears! Just sweaty red faces sporting proud smiles. Running the Daily Mile hadn't just made our children fitter, it had made them more resilient.

Hindu squats

I was watching a TED Talk by Dr John Ratey and was fascinated when he started by getting the audience to perform some 'Hindu squats'. Then, as they sat down, smiling and breathless, Ratey announced, 'Now you're ready to learn.' (Ratey, 2012) Ever since watching that talk, I have used Hindu squats in the classroom to give my class a break and a reboot for their brain. Here is how they work:

- Before they begin, ask the children to place one hand in the middle of their chest and notice their resting heart rate and their normal breathing. Do this for a few breaths.

- Then, ensure the children stand, tuck their chairs under and have enough space to perform the Hindu squats.

- They start by standing straight, with their arms outstretched in front of them (see Figure 9.2 on the next page).

- As the teacher calls out, 'One!', the children pull their arms and elbows back towards their bodies whilst calling out, 'Boom!' (Figure 9.3). Saying 'Boom!' is just a bit of fun.

- They then squat down, touch the floor (Figure 9.4) and stand back up with their arms stretched out, ready for the next Hindu squat.

- Repeat these steps ten times.

- After ten Hindu squats have been completed, ask the children to place one hand in the middle of their chest again to notice how hard their hearts are beating and how quick their breathing is. Just this short burst of exercise is enough to get their brains turned on and the happy hormones flowing.

Go Noodle

A newly qualified teacher called Rachel introduced me to the resource, *Go Noodle* (NQTs often have some of the freshest ideas!). I was walking past her classroom and noticed her class on their feet and moving their bodies to the instructions of Maximo, *Go Noodle*'s on-screen animated monkey. The children were all engaged and having a 'brain-break' in the middle of a lesson. *Go Noodle* describes itself as 'Movement for the

Figure 9.2: Hindu squats step 1

Figure 9.3: Hindu squats step 2 (shout 'Boom!')

Figure 9.4: Hindu squats step 3

Classroom – hundreds of videos to activate kids' bodies and brains.' (**www.gonoodle.com**) Here is what I like about *Go Noodle*:

- it is free to sign-up and use

- lots of the videos are educational (raps about the water cycle, anyone?)

- they're fun and engaging (I challenge you not to join in with the 'How to Dab!' dance video)

- they get children moving

- they're short and, at only two to four minutes in length, they are perfect for mini-breaks during your day.

Visit **www.gonoodle.com** to sign up for free and explore the vast array of videos they have available.

Yoga

If you want your children to experience and practise yoga, the best way to do this effectively is to get a qualified yoga instructor in to teach the children. A good place to start is to search for a local teacher on the British

Wheel of Yoga website (**www.bwy.org.uk/find-a-yoga-class**). Here are some things to bear in mind:

- Decide how you will fund hiring a private yoga instructor. You can use the Sports Premium funding to hire external providers but these classes will need to be in addition to your normal PE lessons (i.e. before school, at lunchtime or after school). Some schools use Pupil Premium funding too and parents could be asked to make a small contribution if necessary.

- Find a local teacher who is experienced at working with children, has current DBS paperwork in place (the Disclosure Barring Service ensures checks are made to confirm adults are safe to work with children), and full public liability insurance.

- Meet with any instructor before you hire them and interview them. Ask them to teach a lesson as part of their interview and observe how they interact with the children. Ensure they are a right fit for your school.

As well as hiring qualified yoga instructors to teach the children in your school, there are some things teachers can do in class. *Go Noodle* has a range of 'stretch' videos based on some basic yoga moves (**app. gonoodle.com/categories/stretch**). The children simply follow the instructions and movements shown on the video, and you can join in as well.

If you're interested in training to teach yoga in school, then **yogaatschool.org.uk** offers training for teachers with their own yoga practice.

Dance

Dancing is as instinctive to humans as storytelling. Who can hear an infectious rhythm or beat and not start tapping their foot or nodding their head? Teaching children how to dance is a whole other ball game though! Once again, *Go Noodle* comes up trumps as they have a dedicated guided dance section (**app.gonoodle.com/categories/ guided-dance**). These are short videos that involve a song to learn and some simple dance moves to copy. My personal favourites are the videos by Blazer Fresh – a young hip-hop trio who remind me of De La Soul.

Another excellent resource is the BBC School Radio primary dance website (**www.bbc.co.uk/schoolradio/subjects/dance**). Teachers can play the audio files, which guide the children through the dance moves and routines. Many of the lessons are cross-curricular, so children can learn about the Great Fire of London, the First World War, the Tudors or even computer coding via the medium of dance!

Key points

- Children are taking part in less physical activity, and becoming more sedentary and obese. This lifestyle behaviour can lead to adult health problems such as type 2 diabetes, heart disease and even premature death.

- Increasing physical activity and fitness in young people has been proven to not only prevent and reverse the health problems noted above, but also boost levels of mental wellbeing, increase happiness levels and longevity, and help improve pupils' academic attainment too.

- Schools can introduce the Daily Mile at little or no cost at all, to get children moving on a daily basis. Children get to improve their fitness, socialise with their friends, and prepare their brains for learning.

- Teachers can easily incorporate more movement into their lessons by using Hindu squats or other short-burst exercises to break up the day. *Go Noodle* has some great interactive videos to get your class moving.

- Yoga has been shown to really help young people's mental wellbeing, so why not find a local teacher to give lessons in your school? Teachers can use simple stretching techniques in class as well.

- Use dance and choreographed movement to help children learn about other areas of the curriculum. Not only will the children get their heart rates up, but the learning of coordinated moves will increase brain plasticity.

Chapter 10
Teacher wellbeing

Thousands of candles can be lit by a single candle and the life of the candle will not be shortened. Happiness never decreases by being shared.
— the Buddha

Chapter overview

In this chapter, we'll learn why it is vital for teachers to prioritise their own wellbeing and how, in doing so, we can improve pupil wellbeing too. We'll look at what can get in the way of teacher wellbeing, and then discover the practical steps we can take to thrive and not just survive in teaching.

In theory	In action
• Put your oxygen mask on first	• Applying the lessons to your own life
• Why teacher wellbeing is important	• Simplify
• Good-enough teaching	• Flex appeal
• Perfectionism	• Nourishing or depleting?
• Shifting old habits	• When you feel swamped
	• Humour
	• Perspective
	• Be courageous

In theory

Put your oxygen mask on first

If you have ever been on a plane, during the safety briefing, the flight attendants will always instruct you to place your oxygen mask on first before helping others, particularly children. The reason makes perfect sense – if you run out of oxygen, you can't help anyone. This is a poignant metaphor for teachers who are charged with the education and nurture of young people. If you truly want to help the children in your care, you must take care of your own wellbeing first. To prioritise your own wellbeing is certainly not a selfish act. As the old saying goes, 'You cannot pour from an empty cup.'

Prioritising your own wellbeing may involve letting go of your instinct for selflessness (and, dare I say it, martyrdom!). We all know a teacher who, no matter what has happened to them, or how ill or injured they are, will turn up to teach regardless. If we're honest, we've probably all been that teacher at some stage in our career. I remember early on when I'd just started teaching, I injured my back playing football outside of school. I woke up in the morning and my back had gone into spasm and I physically couldn't get out of bed. My first thought was, 'Oh no, it's the Year 2 SATs this week – I must get in to be there for my class!' Somehow, I rolled out of bed and crawled on all fours to my phone to call school to say I might be a bit late. Dosed up on enough painkillers to sedate a horse, I stumbled into school and set up my room ready for my class to take their tests. Looking back, I now see how ridiculous that was. Not only did I risk making my back injury far worse, but it was down to me when the Year 2 SATs took place, so I could have called in sick and moved the tests to the following week!

There is no getting away from the fact that teaching is an inherently stressful job. In fact, recent figures published by the Health and Safety Executive show that teaching is one of the most stressful careers there is (Health and Safety Executive, 2017, p. 2). This means that teachers need to take *extra* care of themselves to protect them from the corrosive effects of chronic stress. And although schools play a large role in affecting a teacher's levels of happiness and wellbeing, I believe your wellbeing is too important to be left in the hands of someone other than yourself. In the rest of this chapter, you will learn how you can take proactive steps to look after yourself, in order for you to flourish inside and outside of school.

Why teacher wellbeing is important

As discussed in the introduction to this book (p. 1), teacher wellbeing is at a crisis point in the UK. With record numbers seeking medical advice for stress, and a third leaving teaching within five years of qualifying, it is vital that teachers and schools start to take the issue seriously. Here are three key reasons for why *teacher* wellbeing should be a priority for schools:

1. Role models

Any teacher who wishes to teach happiness and wellbeing to children must first be a role model for happiness and wellbeing. A report on mental health commissioned by the government in 2008 stated that, 'Teachers who are stressed, or demoralised, make poor role models for young people.' (Foresight Mental Capital and Wellbeing Project, 2008) We learned in Chapter 1 (p. 14), from child psychologist Alison Gopnik that children learn more from caregivers' unconscious behaviours and how they act, rather than anything they consciously teach them, so I believe we have to behave and act in a way that models health and wellbeing to our pupils. This is not about teachers being perfect role models, or feeling 'happy' the whole time, or always smiling and being positive in front of pupils. That would be inauthentic and unrealistic. Teachers are allowed to be human and experience the full range of emotions. I'm also not proposing that you need to eat organic salads, know all the asanas of yoga and live a completely Zen lifestyle. Being a role model for wellbeing simply means that teachers show that they take care *of* themselves and care *about* themselves, just as much as they care for their pupils.

2. Pupil success

There is evidence that when teachers look after themselves more, their pupils do better academically. In a review of evidence carried out by Lancaster University and the Teacher Support Network entitled, *Healthy teachers, higher marks?*, it makes a strong case for schools really looking after their key resource – teachers. The report notes that across many industries, employees with high wellbeing are more productive, their quality of work is better, they're more creative and they generally perform better too. The review cites evidence that shows a 'statistically significant positive relationship between staff wellbeing and student SAT outcomes.' (Bajorek et al., 2014) However, when employee wellbeing is low, work performance drops and absences increase. In 2015–16, a staggering 2.16 million days were lost to teacher absences in the UK (Department for Education, 2017a). Another report entitled, *Staff wellbeing is key to school success*, suggests that a virtuous circle is likely to arise in schools when teachers are happy and healthy, and pupils are doing well. The report states, 'There is a two-way relationship between teacher wellbeing and pupil performance…increases in teacher wellbeing can lead to improvements in the performance of pupils, so increases in pupil performance may lead to increased wellbeing in teachers.' (Briner and Dewberry, 2007)

3. This is your life

Teachers' happiness matters because it is important in and of itself. Just as pupils' wellbeing is more important than their grades, so too is your wellbeing. When you start to view your happiness as 'the ultimate currency', then everything changes. It means you naturally start to look for ways to make teaching more meaningful and pleasurable for you and your pupils. You start to do less of the stuff that saps the life out of you and more of the stuff that makes you come alive. Teaching then becomes a source of happiness and you are far more likely to enjoy a long and sustainable teaching career.

Good-enough teaching

Back in the 1950s, English paediatrician and psychoanalyst Donald Winnicott coined the term 'good-enough mothering' (Winnicott, 1962) to describe a mother who does a good-enough job in an extremely complex, difficult and constantly evolving arena. The 'good-enough' mother does her best to attend and attune to her baby's needs but will not always get it right. The 'misattunements' help her child realise that he or she is a separate person from mum and also gives them opportunities to learn how to handle difficulties. Perfection is not an option because not only is it impossible to be a perfect mother, but it also denies the child important developmental processes (such as learning how to be an independent individual and cope with the trials and tribulations of life).

I believe there is a need in education for the 'good-enough teacher', particularly in response to the tyranny of the 'outstanding teacher' (which is a form of perfectionism, in my opinion). The good-enough teacher does their best to care for and educate their class. They always try to make their lessons interesting and engaging. The good-enough teacher aims to develop a love of learning in their pupils and help them reach their full potential. They aim to provide a safe and secure learning environment for their class, and respond to children's physical, emotional and spiritual needs. They want their children to be happy and enjoy coming to school. But sometimes they will get it wrong. Some lessons may be a bit dull. Tiredness may mean the good-enough teacher can be grouchy at times, and not as warm and responsive as they normally are. Good-enough teachers may even, from time to time, yearn for an escape from the huge responsibility they have. But, overall, they enjoy being a teacher, they believe in what they are doing and they do a good job. The blips and mistakes are all accepted as part of being a good-enough teacher and, ultimately, being human.

Perfectionism

One of the things that gets in the way of being 'good enough' is striving for perfection. On my graduation day from my teacher training course, a senior lecturer said to the audience of newly qualified teachers, 'If you are a perfectionist, either change yourself or you may need to change careers.' I remember the advice clearly but didn't quite heed it at first. I also remember thinking to myself, 'You could have told us this a year ago!' In the past, I have tried to be the perfect teacher. I spent ages planning my lessons, scouring the web for the best resources around. I would always be thinking about teaching outside of school and on the lookout for ideas to bring into class. I would tirelessly try to tick off everything from my to-do list each day (not realising that this is impossible!). Every observation I had, or book scrutiny, I aimed for 'outstanding'. I would also stay at school later than necessary, marking in detail to please management and parents. The problem was, this was unsustainable and unrealistic. Not only was I putting myself under massive unnecessary pressure and stress, but by aiming for extrinsic rewards and recognition, I also lost sight of the intrinsic joy of being a teacher.

Studies show that perfectionism can be a barrier to happiness. Psychologist Barry Schwartz and colleagues have done research into people who are either 'maximisers' or 'satisficers' (Schwartz et al., 2002).

Maximisers are perfectionists who always try to seek the best, whereas satisficers are content with what is good enough. It turns out that maximisers are less happy than satisficers for two main reasons:

1. They tend to have more regrets about the *other* choices or decisions they could have made ('That lesson was a bit flat! I wish I'd used those other resources now!').

2. They compare themselves to others more. When given the same task as a peer, their happiness is greatly affected by whether they did better or worse than their peer. ('I can't believe their lesson was graded "outstanding" and mine just "good"!')

Perfectionism may be one reason that teachers leave the profession. Louis Cozolino notes, 'Teachers with the highest levels of commitment and idealistic expectations when they enter the profession are more likely to burn out or leave the field.' (Cozolino, 2013, p. 127) Maybe it is time that more teachers aimed to be good enough and more like satisficers. This isn't about becoming complacent or being happy with mediocrity. The good-enough, satisfied teacher aims to do their best but is wise enough not to aim for perfection. They understand that teaching well is about making mistakes and continually learning, developing and honing their craft. Nor do they seek constant approval from others. Being good enough and satisfied means stripping away layers of unnecessary stresses and pressures that get in the way of the innate pleasure and purpose of teaching.

Shifting old habits

I once read that there is no such thing as getting rid of habits. You simply replace old ones with new ones. But establishing new habits isn't always easy because we often fall back on our default ways of behaving.

However, the Behavioural Insights Team UK have shown that if you want to encourage a new behaviour, you need to make it 'easy, attractive, social and timely' – they call it EAST. (Service et al., 2015) They also note that only small changes and shifts are needed to have big results, so don't feel you need to overhaul your entire life to improve your wellbeing. Small and manageable change is the key to success, and it normally takes around two months for a new habit to become set (Lally et al., 2010).

Let's look at what EAST could mean if, say, a teacher wanted to increase the amount of physical exercise they were getting:

- **Easy**: Try to reduce the 'hassle factor' of the new behaviour. If you want to behave a certain way, pave out the path of least resistance for yourself. Also, harness the power of defaults. People have a strong tendency to go with the default option, so making an option the default makes it more likely to be adopted. Conversely, if you want to stop a certain behaviour, make it harder for yourself to do it. You could, for example, leave your gym kit by the front door the night before, take your running shoes to school and join in with the Daily Mile, or cancel your bus or train ticket and walk or cycle to school.

- **Attractive**: We are more likely to do something that attracts our attention, is novel, or seems appealing and relevant to us. You could watch the '23 and ½ hours' visual lecture by Dr Mike Evans (**www. youtube.com/watch?v=aUaInS6HIGo**), which highlights the huge gains you can expect from exercising more, then go for a run. Alternatively, you could treat yourself to a shiny new bike or some fancy trainers to encourage you to exercise more – the newness of the equipment will make you want to use it, and if you keep it up for eight weeks, a new habit should have set in.

- **Social**: We are highly social creatures and often behave in ways that are similar to others. If we see other people do something, we're more likely to adopt that behaviour ourselves. We are also more likely to do something when we have made a promise to someone else to do it. If you wanted to start doing yoga, for example, you could join a yoga group in your local area – being part of a group will increase your chances of going each week. You could also tell a friend you're starting yoga and this would make you more likely to turn up. Or you could see if your colleagues are interested in doing this too and find a yoga teacher to run a class in your school.

- **Timely**: Our success at adopting a new behaviour varies greatly depending on *when* we choose to do it. Behaviour is easier to change when our habits are disrupted by big life events (such as moving house, changing jobs, getting married or having a child). It might be best to make changes at the start of a new school year. The six-week summer holiday will have broken you out of old habits, so you can start afresh with new intentions. Also, you could choose to exercise at the same time each day or week to establish a new routine, making it a default habit.

In action

Applying the lessons to your own life

Hopefully, as you have been reading about how you can teach children to be happier, you have also been reflecting on how the lessons and techniques in this book can be applied to your own life as well. Maybe reading about tribal classrooms (p. 11) has made you think about creating more of a sense of team in the staffroom. You might have thought about setting up a wellbeing team to focus on staff happiness (regular staff nights out, anyone?). Or after reading about 'what went well' (p. 45), you might have decided to treat yourself to a nice new journal to write down three good things each day before you go to bed. Reflection and thinking about the ideas is great, but if you want to work at boosting your levels of wellbeing, it is going to take *action*. When you start to prioritise happiness and wellbeing, you benefit and the children benefit. Your classroom starts to become a place of refuge rather than a drain. There are lots of ideas to experiment with but remember to make any changes small and manageable. It would be self-defeating if you attempted all of the ideas in this book and then burnt out trying to prioritise your wellbeing! A key thing to remember, though, is that you have a lot of control over your wellbeing – maybe more than you think. Below are some further ideas to bear in mind and act upon when focusing on your wellbeing.

Simplify

When I switched careers to become a teacher, I couldn't believe how busy and complicated a typical teaching day was. Not only was the school day crammed to the brim with lessons and activities, but also every other week there was an event, a school trip, an important visitor or a special occasion to plan for! Being a busy teacher isn't great for wellbeing. Recent brain scans show that people who spend their days rushing around mindlessly have an amygdala (the primitive part of the brain involved in the fight or flight response – see Chapters 2 and

3, pp. 27–59) that is on 'high alert' (Way et al., 2010). Being busy also means we can feel 'time poor', where we feel we don't have enough time to do all of our tasks. This can leave us feeling rushed, overworked and constantly playing catch-up. But it doesn't have to be this way.

In his book, *Happier*, Tal Ben-Shahar strongly advises that everyone, teacher or otherwise, should simplify their lives. Ben-Shahar states that, 'This means safeguarding our time, learning to say "no" more often – to people as well as opportunities…It means prioritising, choosing activities that we really, really want to do, while letting go of others.' (Ben-Shahar, 2008, p. 154) He also talks about reducing our list of 'have-tos' (things we do, motivated by extrinsic factors like obligation, fear, status or a desire to please) and increasing more of our 'want-tos' (activities that are intrinsically rewarding and give us meaning and pleasure). Ultimately, simplifying your life is about taking control and using your autonomy to carve out a lifestyle that works for you.

I have fully embraced this philosophy. Wherever possible, I try to simplify what I do personally and professionally. At work, I have set clear boundaries for myself and make sure that at least 95 per cent of my schoolwork is carried out at school and not at home. I arrive at school at around 7.45am (I live locally) and leave no later than 5pm. I prioritise my work so important stuff gets done each day and if I am not able to do it before I leave, it can wait. I have sought out simpler ways of working at school and then suggested these to my headteacher. Not all of my ideas were taken on board but embracing simplicity at work has led to my school slimming down our planning requirements, halving the length of our school report template and reducing the number of morning briefing meetings we had from five down to one. All have resulted in staff feeling a lot more time-rich, with more time to do other things. I have also made personal choices like choosing to work part-time to look after my son two days a week, which meant turning down an opportunity to apply for a deputy headteacher role. By simplifying my working life, I feel like my job works for me rather than the other way around.

Two important questions to ask yourself then are:

1. In what ways can I simplify my working life?

2. How can I engineer my life so I get to spend more time on the things I really *want* to do, and less time on the things I feel I *have* to do?

Flex appeal

One way to bring more balance to your life is to work flexibly. Flexible working is basically thinking differently about *how* you work, *when* you work and *where* you work. The four main ways that you can work flexibly are:

1. part-time working (you work reduced hours and are paid pro-rata)
2. job share (one job is split between two or more people, who all work part-time)
3. compressed hours (you work full-time hours but do so in fewer but longer days)
4. working from home (you complete all or some of your work from home).

All employees in the UK now have the statutory right to request to work flexibly and employers have to give the request due consideration. In fact, your school should have a flexible working policy by law. Now, there are some obvious limitations to how flexibly you can work when you have a class to teach. It would be great to work from home and teach your class from the comfort of your sofa, but that isn't going to happen any time soon. However, some schools embrace flexible working by allowing staff to take their planning, preparation and assessment (PPA) time off-site, so this may be something you could request at your school. Depending on when your PPA time is, it could mean coming into school late or leaving early one day a week, which could make a big difference. One school I worked in would give staff a day off in lieu if they ran an after-school club for a term. It meant you could earn up to three 'club days' a year. These came in handy for when teachers wanted long weekends or days off in the middle of term time. The fact is, schools and teachers do not need to be beholden to the outdated industrial structure of nine-to-five, five days a week, and can be more creative with how staff work.

When my wife and I were expecting our first child, his due date was right at the beginning of a school year. Plus, I was starting work at a brand new school! The thought of teaching full time with a newborn baby at home terrified me, so I asked my new headteacher if I could work part-time for the first term. She agreed, and so from September until January, I worked four days a week. That day off with my wife and new baby was a real lifesaver. Not only did it give me some respite in the busy autumn term, but also I got to spend some quality time with my new enlarged family. The following academic year, when my wife returned to work part-time, I requested to work three days a week so I could share childcare with my wife (see Figure 10.1). Again, my headteacher was accommodating and granted me part-time working. My headteacher had the right to turn my request down but the fact is, I asked. If you feel flexible working is something that might help with your work–life balance, then ask your headteacher. You do not need to be a parent to request flexible working. It is worth reading this guidance from the Department for Education about flexible working, so you know your rights and your school's responsibilities: **www.gov.uk/government/publications/flexible-working-in-schools** (Department

Figure 10.1: My son and me enjoying some café culture on one of my 'days off' (a day with a toddler isn't really a day off but I still love it!)

for Education, 2017b). Also, organisations like **www.timewise.co.uk** are on a mission to make flexible working the norm in all sectors, so check them out too.

Nourishing or depleting?

It can be really helpful to audit what we do on a daily basis and see which activities motivate us and which ones sap us of energy. Based on a practice from *Mindfulness-Based Cognitive Therapy for Depression* (Seagal et al., 2002), a useful activity to do is called 'nourishing or depleting'. Here is how it works:

- First, bring to mind all the activities you do on a typical day, starting from when you wake up, to when you go to sleep.

- Next, write these down in a list.

- Now, consider each activity and decide which ones give you energy, make you feel good or lift your mood. These are nourishing activities, so put an 'N' next to these ones.

- Then, consider which activities drain you, leave you feeling stressed or frazzled, or pull you down. These are depleting ones, so put a 'D' next to these ones. If an activity is both, or you can't decide, you can put 'N/D' next to them. The table below gives an example of how a list may start.

It can be quite revealing to realise how many of our activities drain and deplete us. This isn't meant to upset you but to help you bring more awareness to how you live day-to-day. Your list does not even have to be in perfect balance, as one nourishing activity that really energises you

Daily activities	Nourishing or depleting?
Alarm goes off	D
Shower	N
Get dressed	N
Eat breakfast and watch news	N/D
Drive to school	D
Set up classroom	N/D
Check emails	D

can outweigh several smaller depleting ones. Once you have a good idea of how your daily activities affect you, ask yourself these two questions:

1. How can I turn depleting or neutral activities into more nourishing ones? It could be a simple thing like changing your alarm tone from a harsh beep to a more melodic one, or turning off the news whilst you eat breakfast, or having your favourite music playing as you set up your classroom. Experiment with small, subtle changes and see what impact they have.

2. How can I incorporate more nourishing activities into my day? Maybe you choose to take part in an activity that gives you flow (see Chapter 6, p. 93), take up an old hobby, go for a nice meal or call a good friend for a chat. Try to have a bank of nourishing activities you can dip into and attempt to do at least one a day to add more balance to your life.

When you feel swamped

Often when we are most stressed, busy or exhausted we become paralysed and don't know what to do to ameliorate our suffering. It can start to feel like you're losing control over your life as the demands of teaching and your personal life take over. But there are some simple things you can do to wrest back some control and regain your sense of agency:

- **Take some deep breaths**: Just pausing and focusing on your breathing for a few minutes can gradually take you out of fight or flight mode.

- **Do something that gives you pleasure**: You can use your bank of nourishing activities for inspiration. Go for a walk, listen to your favourite music, meet up with a friend, take a long bath, have a massage, eat your favourite food or watch a funny film. Doing something just for you can distract you from your worries and nourish you.

- **Complete a small task, any task**: Even just vacuuming a room in your house or renewing your car's MOT can give you a sense of control over your life.

- **Ask for help**: If you are swamped, ask someone for help. You may find that they too are swamped and at least you realise you're not on your own. Don't be afraid of saying to your leadership team that you are struggling with workload, or speaking to friends and family about your worries. The Education Support Partnership (**www. educationsupportpartnership.org.uk**), who give mental health and wellbeing support to teaching staff, have a free helpline – 08000 562 561. Asking for help is a courageous act and not something to be ashamed of.

Humour

Laughing is one of the fastest ways to counteract tension and stress. Not only does your body flood with happy hormones when you're laughing, which reduces stress levels and makes you feel good, but it is contagious. When you laugh with others it is a shared and bonding experience. It is impossible to feel stressed or overwhelmed when you are laughing! Fortunately for you, primary school teaching gives you no end of humorous material to indulge in. From the funny things children say (like the boy I spent an entire afternoon with trying to help him say the word, 'flamingo', but who kept on saying 'flamango'), to the hilarious things that happen to you (such as the time I joined in with a kickabout in the playground and completely ripped my trousers), your week is full of opportunities to laugh. Make sure you don't let them drift by unnoticed. Savour the funny moments that you share with your class and your colleagues, and try not to take yourself too seriously. In fact, right now, why not try the following activity?

- Bring to mind your all-time top three funniest moments of your teaching career. What happened, who was there and why was it so funny?
- Relive those funny moments by sharing them with a colleague or friend. Laugh until you're crying.
- Repeat often.

Perspective

Stress can also narrow our perspective, causing us to focus only on ourselves and our problems, which can exacerbate how bad our problems seem. It can really help your mental health and wellbeing to consciously widen your perspective at such times. By gaining some perspective, you're able to see your problems more clearly and, perhaps, realise that they're not so bad after all. Here are some techniques to try out when you're feeling particularly under pressure:

- **Consider a problem in relation to the universe**: Watch the video, *The Scale of the Universe* **www.youtube.com/watch?v=nxs5wye0JXs** (Business Insider, 2015) and consider a problem or worry you might have in the context of the universe. Ask yourself, 'In the grand scheme of things, is this really as big and bad as I think it is?'

- **Reconnect with your *Ikigai***: 'Ikigai' is a Japanese expression that roughly translates as your 'reason for being' or 'why you get out of bed in the morning'. So, reflect on *why* you became a teacher. What is it about teaching, or your class, that makes you want to get out of bed in the morning? Reminding yourself of your purpose can be a great way to help you focus on what really matters, rather than dwelling on smaller worries.

- **Stay humble**: It is so easy to get stuck in a rut of bemoaning 'the system', or parents, or the senior leadership team for the various hoops we teachers have to jump through. But, it means we lose sight of how lucky we are to be a primary school teacher. When you stop to take it in, primary school teaching is such a huge privilege. We get to spend our days in the company of the most diverse, interesting, funny, warm and unique human beings on the planet. We have the honour of helping to influence and shape their lives and, in return, they undoubtedly mould and inspire our lives too. Sometimes, when I'm outdoors teaching PE in the sunshine, or inside getting my class to recite their amazing poetry, I think to myself, 'I can't believe I get paid to do this!' See if you can find moments in your week when you genuinely feel lucky to be doing this job, and savour them.

- **Take advice from an older, wiser you**: Imagine yourself in the future, significantly older than you are now. What advice would you give to yourself to help you cope with your current struggles but also to find more happiness in your life right now? Spend ten minutes writing down the advice. If, for example, your older self advises you to spend more time with your friends, see if you can commit to a weekly meet-up with a mate. Does imagining yourself way into the future help you get some perspective on your current worries? Will this issue still be around when you are much older? This activity can enable us to tap into the innate wisdom we already have within us, to help us handle situations more wisely.

Be courageous

When it comes to happiness, many people delay their happy life until the future, falsely believing that they will be happy when some event or thing happens to make life better. A teacher might say, 'Oh, I'll be happier when Ofsted have been and gone, or when this term is over, or once I've completed this project.' But the time for happiness is now! Happiness comes from the day-to-day, the ordinary, even the mundane. As Ben-Shahar comments, 'A happy – or happier – life is rarely shaped by some extraordinary life-changing event; rather, it is shaped incrementally, experience by experience, moment by moment.' (Ben-Shahar, 2008, p. 168) And we *all* have the ability to be the designer and architect of our own happiness.

But to teach happiness and wellbeing at school, and to apply the lessons to your own life, may take courage and may require you to dare to be different. But, my question to you is, what have you got to lose? Therefore, I lay down a challenge before you. Start to mix things up at your school. Prioritise your wellbeing and the children's. Be bold, be brave and experiment. This is your life and your teaching career, so take back control and steer your own ship. Mary Oliver wrote in a poem called *The Summer Day*, 'Tell me, what is it you plan to do with your one wild and precious life?' (Oliver, 1992) So, what is it that you plan to do with yours?

Key points

- It is important for teachers to prioritise their wellbeing because they cannot give to their pupils if they are depleted. If we are good role models for our children, our wellbeing can impact pupil attainment, and our wellbeing matters in and of itself.

- Perfectionism gets in the way of our happiness. Aiming to be simply 'good enough' can help us find pleasure and purpose in teaching.
- If we want to make changes to our behaviour, we should make them easy, attractive, social and timely.
- Teachers can apply all of the lessons in this book to their own lives.
- We can simplify our working lives to free up more time, set boundaries for work and start to feel less pressured. You have the option of requesting to work flexibly to bring more balance to your life.
- Find opportunities to laugh. Humour is a great stress reliever.
- If teachers feel really swamped, doing something pleasurable, completing a task or asking for help can alleviate those pressures.
- Regain perspective by putting your problems in the context of the universe, reconnecting with why you became a teacher, staying humble by appreciating the privilege of being a teacher, and seeking advice from an older, wiser you.
- Be bold and brave with teaching happiness and wellbeing, and with making teaching work for you!

Glossary

Adrenaline – a hormone released by the adrenal glands whose major function is to prepare the body for fight or flight by increasing blood flow to the muscles.

Altruism – when we act to promote someone else's welfare even at a risk or cost to ourselves.

Amygdala – a primeval part of the brain central to emotion and motivation. Its major function is to act as an alarm bell to other areas of the brain and the body when it senses danger by kick-starting the fight or flight response, otherwise known as the **stress response**.

Anxiety reappraisal – when we 'reframe' our anxious feelings as 'excitement' during nerve-wracking activities. Studies show that this can help us to perform better.

Attachment – the term psychologists use to describe 'love'. Our levels of attachment are strongly influenced by the nurture and care we received as infants. We can grow up with attachment styles that are 'secure', 'avoidant', 'anxious', or 'disorganised'.

Autopilot – a state of mind where we do things automatically, without thinking about them. When our brain learns something well, it automates it, freeing up vital brain power and energy to focus on other things. When we operate on 'autopilot', we are not being mindful.

BDNF – brain-derived neurotrophic factor (BDNF) helps build and maintain brain circuitry. It improves the functions of neurons, encourages their growth, and strengthens and protects them against the natural process of cell death.

Compassion – the ability to sense another's suffering and then feeling compelled to try to relieve their suffering.

Cortisol – a stress hormone that is released by the adrenal glands, along with adrenaline, during the stress response. In large doses, cortisol makes you hyper vigilant, halts your immune system, stops your ability to learn and prevents you from relaxing.

Dopamine – a hormone and neurotransmitter that helps us pay attention, and is part of our 'reward system' – that is, when something good happens to us, we get a rush of dopamine that makes us feel good. It gets released when we achieve something, when we exercise and, also, when we laugh and find something amusing.

Empathy – the ability to sense other people's emotions and think about what others may be thinking or feeling.

Endorphins – hormones and neurotransmitters that help protect us against stress, reduce our experience of pain and produce pleasure. They are often released during exercise, hence the 'high' runners feel after a run.

Flow – a state of mind we experience when we are fully absorbed in an activity that challenges us. When we are in flow, we often lose sense of ourselves and time feels like it rushes by. Experiencing flow benefits our wellbeing.

Happy hormones – hormones that positively contribute to our physical and mental health, which are released by the body when we partake in particular behaviours or have certain experiences (see also **dopamine**, **endorphins**, **oxytocin** and **serotonin**).

Hippocampus – a part of the brain central to forming new memories (especially spatial memories). It is also involved with putting things in perspective and calming down the **amygdala** (see above) when necessary. New neurons are born in the hippocampus.

Kindness – a general term that means being friendly, helpful and generous towards others (psychologists often call it 'prosocial' behaviour).

Meta-cognition – the ability to be aware of your thinking and able to regulate it. It also involves knowledge of when and how to use particular strategies for learning and problem solving.

Mindfulness – paying attention to what's happening in the present moment in the mind, body and external environment, with an attitude of kindness and curiosity.

Mirror neurons – discovered by neurophysiologist Giacomo Rizzolatti, mirror neurons fire when we carry out an action or witness someone else carry out an action and they might move us to imitate what we observe. They are also thought to be partly responsible for our ability to empathise with other people and feel what they are feeling.

Negativity bias – the default nature of our brains to look out for dangers and spot threats easily, so as to avoid them in the future. Our brains are better at storing and remembering negative events because of this.

Neural Darwinism – some neurons form connections that stay intact and become strong, whereas others do not and die off in a process that resembles natural selection. The strongest and most adaptable neurons and connections survive in a battle of survival of the fittest.

Neurons – a cell in the brain that sends and receives signals to and from other neurons. Each neuron has one axon (axons are the main way by which neurons pass information on and *teach* other neurons) and up to 100,000 dendrites (which are the main way by which neurons get information and *learn* from other neurons).

Neuroplasticity – the brain's ability to continually change and adapt in response to thoughts, actions and experiences.

Neurotransmitters – chemicals and hormones that allow neurons to send messages to one another. Happy hormones are a type of neurotransmitter that contributes to our sense of happiness and wellbeing (see **happy hormones**).

Optimism – the expectation that the future will be socially desirable, good and pleasurable.

Oxytocin – a hormone and neurotransmitter that promotes prosocial behaviour and bonding between people. It helps us to be kind and show empathy towards others. It causes the release of nitric oxide, which helps lower blood pressure, as well as reducing the volume of free radicals in our system (responsible for ageing and tissue damage) and reducing inflammation of our cardiovascular system.

Pessimism – the expectation that the future will be socially undesirable, negative and uncomfortable.

Positive psychology – the study of how human beings flourish and what contributes to a happy and meaningful life.

Pre-frontal cortex – the part of the brain that sets goals, makes plans and directs action. It is also responsible for **meta-cognition** (see above), regulating behaviour and abstract thinking.

Priming – influencing people to think and behave in desirable ways by use of a stimulus (such as exposure to nature or a positive message).

Prosocial behaviour – (see **kindness**)

Psychological wellbeing – a person's sense of meaning, purpose and engagement with life.

Reframing – when we take a negative situation and 'reframe' it by consciously adopting a positive perspective.

REM sleep – rapid eye movement sleep is a period of sleep in which we typically dream. It is thought to be when our short-term memories get moved over to our long-term memory.

Sedentary behaviour – any behaviour that involves sitting or lying down for extended periods of time.

Serotonin – a hormone and neurotransmitter that regulates our mood, sleep and digestion. When people suffer from depression, any antidepressants they are given aim to boost its effects. Our diet can affect our levels of serotonin as can our exposure to natural light. Eating well and getting outdoors are two ways to help regulate our serotonin levels.

Signature strengths – the character strengths (such as kindness, love of learning, humour, curiosity, bravery and honesty) that are most essential to who we are. They drive our thoughts, feelings and behaviours and are what motivate us.

Stress response – when we perceive a threat or sense danger, our bodies prepare for fight or flight. Our **amygdala** senses the threat and sends a message to the adrenal glands to release **cortisol** and **adrenaline** (see above). Our heart rate increases and our pupils dilate as we prepare for action.

Stretch zone – a state in which our skills, abilities and aptitudes are stretched to their limits and when we feel outside our comfort zone. We learn best when we are in our stretch zone but if we are pushed too far, we enter the 'panic zone' where learning stops and we become overwhelmed.

Subjective wellbeing – a person's own assessment of how well their life, or specific aspects of it, are going. Two commonly used measures of 'subjective wellbeing' are life satisfaction and the experience of positive and negative emotions.

Tribal classroom – a classroom that taps into children's innate tribal instincts by creating a safe, secure learning environment, and a sense of belonging to a team or family. Tribal classrooms are democratic and inclusive and they encourage laughter, exploration and play.

Further reading and recommended resources

Below I have suggested some further reading materials if you would like to explore further the topics and themes touched upon in each chapter. I also recommend websites and courses related to teaching happiness and wellbeing.

Chapter 1: Creating a tribal classroom

The Social Neuroscience of Education: Optimizing Attachment and Learning in the Classroom by Louis Cozolino – a fantastic book that I believe all teachers would benefit from reading. It is great at explaining the neuroscience behind learning and gives examples of teachers who have established tribal classrooms in their own unique way.

The Gardener and the Carpenter: What the New Science of Child Development Tells Us About the Relationship Between Parents and Children by Alison Gopnik – this book challenges how many of us teach, parent and raise our children today. A good book for teachers as it shows how children develop, why play is so important and what children need most to help them to flourish.

Chapter 2: Mindfulness

Mindfulness: A Practical Guide to Finding Peace in a Frantic World by Mark Williams and Danny Penman – this is my go-to book for anything mindfulness related. Really well-written and engaging, it clearly explains what mindfulness is and how it can help people cope with the stresses of everyday life. It even has an eight-week mindfulness course you can follow along with a CD containing guided meditations.

Sitting Still Like a Frog: Mindfulness Exercises for Kids (and Their Parents) by Eline Snel – a lovely short book that explains mindfulness well for children to understand. Plus, it has some fun exercises to try, as well as a CD with guided meditations. I often play the 'A Safe Place' meditation because you get to lie down – a great one for a Friday in class!

Peaceful Piggy Meditation and *Moody Cow Meditates* by Kerry Lee Maclean – two picture books that show children how meditation can help us cope with difficult feelings and emotions that come up in everyday life. They have guided meditations and activities at the back of the book.

100 Ideas for Primary Teachers: Mindfulness in the Classroom by Tammie Prince – this is a great little book packed with ideas for bringing mindfulness practices and activities to life in your classroom.

Chapter 3: What went well?

Hardwiring Happiness: How to Reshape Your Brain and Your Life by Rick Hanson – of the many books on happiness that I have read, this is one I keep coming back to. Hanson really gets to the route of how to make happy experiences become hardwired in our brains, and there are some great meditations and exercises to try to help you grow your happiness.

Thanks! How Practicing Gratitude Can Make You Happier by Robert Emmons – Emmons is the expert on gratitude and this book explains the science behind why practising it makes you happier, as well as giving lots of practical ideas.

Chapter 4: Neuroplasticity – your elastic plastic brain

A User's Guide to the Brain by Dr John Ratey – a must-read if you are interested in how our brains work. It is extremely comprehensive and is accessible for the neuroscience novice.

Buddha's Brain: The Practical Neuroscience of Happiness, Love and Wisdom by Rick Hanson – this book uses modern neuroscience to shine a light on ancient contemplative practices to show how they actually change our brains and shape our thoughts. A very insightful book.

The Emotional Life of Your Brain: How its Unique Patterns Affect the Way You Think, Feel, and Live – and How You Can Change Them by Richard Davidson and Sharon Begley – this book explains how our brains give us our own unique 'emotional style' and that we can learn to change these to serve us better.

Your Fantastic Elastic Brain: Stretch it, Shape it by JoAnn Deak – a great picture book for children that really helps them understand neuroplasticity and why mistakes are good for your brain.

What Goes On In My Head? How Your Brain Works and Why You Do What You Do By Robert Winston – a wonderful book to help children understand how amazing their brains are. Packed with loads of facts and interesting insights.

Chapter 5: The stretch zone

Mindset: Changing the Way You Think to Fulfil Your Potential by Carol Dweck – apparently growth mindset is one of the most talked about topics in teaching at the moment, but very few people have actually read Carol Dweck's book. If you really want to know your stuff on growth mindset, this is your first port of call.

Happier: Can You Learn to be Happy? by Tal Ben-Shahar – this book has a whole chapter on education and will really help you reflect on your teaching practice.

Chapter 6: Flow and strengths

Flow: The Psychology of Happiness by Mihaly Csikszentmihalyi – the undisputed expert on flow, Csikszentmihalyi explains what it is and how it could be an unsung yet key component of happiness.

Flourish: A New Understanding of Happiness and Wellbeing – and How to Achieve Them by Martin Seligman – Seligman started the positive psychology movement and this book shares his research and wisdom but in a conversational and engaging way that isn't bogged down with science or data.

Chapter 7: It's cool to be kind

Do Nice, Be Kind, Spread Happy: Acts of Kindness for Kids by Bernadette Russell – some great ideas for children on what they could do for their random acts of kindness. They'll learn how to be a 'niceness ninja and a happiness hero'.

A Force For Good: The Dalai Lama's Vision for Our World by Dan Goleman – Goleman shares the Dalai Lama's vision for humanity in this heart-warming and inspiring book. A good book to read to help restore your faith in humanity.

Chapter 8: How our thoughts shape our world

Happiness By Design: Finding Pleasure and Purpose in Everyday Life by Professor Paul Dolan – happiness doesn't have to be hard work according to Dolan. In this book, he promotes 'easy' proven ways to positively impact your wellbeing, and shares some of the research on 'priming'. A great read with lots of 'happiness hacks'.

Chapter 9: Exercise makes me happy

Spark! How Exercise Will Improve the Performance of Your Brain by Dr John Ratey – I thought I knew a lot about how exercise affects our brains until I read this book. Ratey shares the latest research on just how powerful and crucial exercise is for our brains, health and happiness.

Chapter 10: Teacher wellbeing

How To Survive in Teaching: Without Imploding, Exploding or Walking Away by Dr Emma Kell – Emma is a teacher with over 20 years' experience. In her brilliant book she shares her wisdom and research on what drives teachers away from the profession and also, helpfully, what practical things teachers can do to look after themselves and each other more, so they can enjoy rewarding and long-lasting careers.

General books on happiness

Happier: Can You Learn to be Happy? by Tal Ben-Shahar – so good it gets a second mention. It is one of the best books I have read on the subject of happiness. So much is packed into such a small book and it is all relevant and helpful.

10 Keys to Happier Living: A Practical Handbook for Happiness by Vanessa King – very practical with lots of ideas to experiment with. It is so thorough and easy to dip in and out of.

50 Ways to Feel Happy by Vanessa King, Peter Harper and Val Payne – an excellent book aimed at children. Basically, a children's version of King's book above. It is beautifully illustrated, very engaging and full of practical activities for children to try out to grow their happiness.

Happiness: Lessons From a New Science by Lord Richard Layard – in terms of people trying to get wellbeing on the national agenda in relation to politics, economics and education, Layard is a pioneer in this country.

Websites

www.ipen-network.com – home of the International Positive Education Network. Sign up to access great resources, receive their newsletter and to find out when their excellent conferences are.

www.annafreud.org/what-we-do/schools-in-mind – The Anna Freud National Centre for Children and Families has created 'Schools In Mind', which is a free network that provides an excellent range of accessible information and evidence-based resources that schools, teachers and support staff can use to support the mental health and wellbeing of the children and young people in their care.

www.mindfulnessinschools.org – a charity leading the way in terms of training educational professionals in delivering mindfulness curriculums in schools.

www.greatergood.berkeley.edu – sign up to receive their articles on the latest research on the science of happiness.

www.viacharacter.org/www – for any research or work on character strengths, this is the website to use.

www.foodafactoflife.org.uk/attachments/ca2d5f8c-df84-4a678354f616.pdf – a selection of lesson plans to teach your children more about the importance of food and diet.

www.teachappy.co.uk – to find out more about the work I'm doing in schools, or to read my blog, please check out my website, or follow me on Twitter @AdrianBethune.

Courses

Action for Happiness: *Keys to Happier Living Toolkit for Schools* (by Peter Harper and Val Payne) – **www.actionforhappiness.org/toolkit** – an engaging and accessible, evidence-based programme to promote the emotional wellbeing and resilience of children aged seven to 11.

Seeds of Happiness – together with Young Happy Minds co-founder, Yvonne Biggins (MAPP), I have created a six-week course in positive psychology for primary school children. Go to **www.teachappy. co.uk/positive-psychology** to find out more.

Teaching Happiness – course by ICEPE **http://icepe.eu/cpd/ Teaching_Happiness** – an online course for teachers and education professionals who want to learn more about how they can apply positive psychology in the classroom.

Measuring wellbeing

From my experience, most schools do not know where to begin when it comes to measuring staff and pupil wellbeing in a meaningful way. Fortunately, there are some great resources out there to help you in this endeavour.

Pupil wellbeing

The Anna Freud National Centre for Children and Families has created a toolkit for schools that wish to begin to measure and monitor their pupils' mental wellbeing. They have even created a FREE eLearning course to increase your understanding, knowledge and confidence of measuring pupil wellbeing. Follow the link to download the toolkit and sign up to the course – **www.annafreud.org/what-we-do/schools-in-mind/ resources-for-schools/mental-health-toolkit-for-schools**

Staff wellbeing

The Education Support Partnership has developed a 'Positive Workplace Survey' to help schools measure staff wellbeing and also a 'Positive Workplace Programme' where they can design a plan for school improvement based on the survey results. This is not a free service, but it is well worth the money! Go to **www.educationsupportpartnership. org.uk/staff-engagement-wellbeing**

Bibliography

Achor, S. (2011), *The Happiness Advantage: The Seven Principles of Positive Psychology that Fuel Success and Performance at Work*. London: Virgin Books.

Aknin, L. B., Barrington-Leigh, C. P., Dunn, E. W., Helliwell, J. F., Burns, J., Biswas-Diener, R., Kemeza, I., Nyende, P. and Ashton-James, C. E. (2013a), 'Prosocial spending and well-being: cross-cultural evidence for a psychological universal', *Journal of Personality and Social Psychology*, 104, (4), 635–52.

Aknin, L. B., Dunn, E. W., Whillans, A. V., Grant, A. M., and Norton, M. I. (2013b), 'Making a difference matters: impact unlocks the emotional benefits of prosocial spending', *Journal of Economic Behavior and Organization*, 88, 90–5.

Aknin, L. B., Sandstrom, G. M., Dunn, E. W. and Norton, M. I. (2011), 'It's the recipient that counts: spending money on strong social ties leads to greater happiness than spending on weak social ties', *PLoS ONE*, 6, (2), e17018.

American Psychological Association (2017), 'Secret to happiness may include more unpleasant emotions', **www.apa.org/news/press/releases/2017/08/secret-happiness.aspx**

Babyak, M., Blumenthal, J. A., Herman, S., Khatri, P., Doraiswamy, M., Moore, K., Craighead, W. E., Baldewicz, T. T. and Krishnan, K. R. (2000), 'Exercise treatment for major depression: maintenance of therapeutic benefit at ten months', *Psychosomatic Medicine*, 62, (5), 633–8.

Bajorek, Z., Gulliford, J. and Taskila, T. (2014), 'Healthy teachers, higher marks? Establishing a link between teacher health and wellbeing, and student outcomes'. London: The Work Foundation (Lancaster University), **www.educationsupportpartnership.org.uk/sites/default/files/resources/healthy_teachers_higher_marks_report_0.pdf**

Barraza, J. A. and Zak, P. J. (2009), 'Empathy toward strangers triggers oxytocin release and subsequent generosity', *Annals of the New York Academy of Sciences*, 1167, 182–9.

Ben-Shahar, T. (2008), *Happier: Can You Learn to be Happy?* New York, NY: McGraw-Hill Education.

Biddle, S., Cavill, N., Ekelund, U., Gorely, T., Griffiths, M., Jago, R., Oppert, J., Raats, M., Salmon, J., Stratton, G., Vicente-Rodríguez, G., Butland,

B., Prosser, L. and Richardson, D. (2010), 'Sedentary behaviour and obesity: review of the current scientific evidence'. London: Department of Health and Department for Children, Schools and Families, **www.gov. uk/government/uploads/system/uploads/attachment_data/file/ 213745/dh_128225.pdf**

Bjork, E. L. and Bjork, R. A. (2001), 'Making things hard on yourself, but in a good way: creating desirable difficulties to enhance learning'. In M. A. Gernsbacher, R. W. Pew, L. M. Hough and J. R. Pomerantz (Eds.), *Psychology and the Real World*, pp. 56–64. New York, NY: Worth Publishers.

Black, S. (2001), 'Morale matters: when teachers feel good about their work, research shows, student achievement rises', *American School Board Journal*, 188, (1), 40–3.

Blackwell, L. S., Trzesniewski, K. H. and Dweck, C. S. (2007), 'Implicit theories of intelligence predict achievement across an adolescent transition: a longitudinal study and an intervention', *Child Development*, 78, (1), 246–63.

Blum, D. (2002), *Love at Goon Park: Harry Harlow and the Science of Affection*. Cambridge, MA: Perseus.

Brickman, P., Coates, D. and Janoff-Bulman, R. (1978), 'Lottery winners and accident victims: is happiness relative?', *Journal of Personality and Social Psychology*, 36, (8), 917–27.

Briffa, J. (2014), *A Great Day at the Office: 10 Simple Strategies for Maximising Your Energy and Getting the Best Out of Yourself and Your Day*. London: Fourth Estate.

Briner, R. and Dewberry, C. (2007), 'Staff wellbeing is key to school success: a research study into the links between staff wellbeing and school performance'. London: Worklife Support, **www. worklifesupport.com/sites/default/files/uploaded-documents/ 5902BirkbeckWBPerfSummaryFinal.pdf**

British Nutrition Foundation (2016), 'Hydration for children', **www. nutrition.org.uk/healthyliving/hydration/hydration-for-children. html**

Brooks, A. W. (2014), 'Get excited: reappraising pre-performance anxiety as excitement', *Journal of Experimental Psychology: General*, 143, (3), 1144–58.

Brown, S. L., Smith, D. M., Schulz, R., Kabeto, M. U., Ubel, P. A. Poulin, M., Yi, J., Kim, C. and Langa, K. M. (2009), 'Caregiving behavior is associated with decreased mortality risk', *Psychological Science*, 20, (4), 488–94.

Business Insider (2015), 'The scale of the universe', **www.youtube.com/ watch?v=nxs5wye0JXs**

Chang, E. C. and Sanna, L. J. (2001), 'Optimism, pessimism, and positive and negative affectivity in middle-aged adults: a test of a cognitive-affective model of psychological adjustment', *Psychology and Aging*, 16, (3), 524–31.

Clark, A. E., Flèche, S., Layard, R., Powdthavee, N. and Ward, G. (2018), *The Origins of Happiness: The Science Of Well-being over the Life Course*. Princeton: Princeton University Press.

Cozolino, L. (2013), *The Social Neuroscience of Education: Optimizing Attachment and Learning in the Classroom*. New York, NY: W.W. Norton & Company.

Cozolino, L. (2014), *Attachment-Based Teaching: Creating a Tribal Classroom*. New York; London: W.W. Norton & Company.

Csikszentmihalyi, M. (1998), *Finding Flow: The Psychology of Engagement With Everyday Life*. New York, NY: Basic Books.

Csikszentmihalyi, M. (2002), *Flow: The Psychology of Happiness*. London: Rider.

Darwin, C. R. (1871), *The Descent of Man, and Selection in Relation to Sex* (Volume 1). London: John Murray.

Davidson, R. J. (2004), 'What does the prefrontal cortex "do" in affect: perspectives on frontal EEG asymmetry research', *Biological Psychology*, 67, (1–2), 219–33.

Davidson, R. J. and Begley, S. (2012), *The Emotional Life of Your Brain: How its Unique Patterns Affect the Way You Think, Feel, and Live – and How You Can Change Them*. London: Hodder and Stoughton.

Davidson, R. J., Kabat-Zinn, J., Schumacher, J., Rosenkranz, M., Muller, D., Santorelli, S. F., Urbanowski, F., Harrington, A., Bonus, K. and Sheridan, J. F. (2003), 'Alterations in brain and immune function produced by mindfulness meditation', *Psychosomatic Medicine*, 65, (4), 564–70.

Department for Education (2017a), 'School Workforce in England: November 2016', Crown Copyright, **www.gov.uk/government/uploads/system/uploads/attachment_data/file/620825/SFR25_2017_MainText.pdf**

Department for Education (2017b), 'Flexible working in schools: guidance to help teachers, schools and employers make arrangements for flexible working', Crown Copyright, **www.gov.uk/government/publications/flexible-working-in-schools**

Diener, E. and Biswas-Diener, R. (2008), *Happiness: Unlocking the Mysteries of Psychological Wealth*. Oxford: Wiley-Blackwell.

Dolan, P. (2015), *Happiness by Design: Finding Pleasure and Purpose in Everyday Life*. London: Penguin.

Dunbar, R. I. M. (1992), 'Neocortex size as a constraint on group size in primates', *Journal of Human Evolution*, 22, (6), 469–93.

Dunn, E. and Norton, M. (2013), *Happy Money: The New Science of Smarter Spending*. London: Oneworld Publications.

Durlak, J. A., Weissberg, R. P., Dymnicki, A. B., Taylor, R. D. and Schellinger, K. B., (2011), 'The impact of enhancing students' social and emotional learning: a meta-analysis of school-based universal interventions', *Child Development*, 82, (1), 405–32.

Dweck, C. S. (2007), 'The perils and promises of praise', *Educational Leadership*, 65, (2), 34–9.

Eisenberg, N. and Fabes, R. A. (1990), 'Empathy: conceptualization, measurement, and relation to prosocial behavior', *Motivation and Emotion*, 14, (2), 131–49.

Ellis, A. (1962), *Reason and Emotion in Psychotherapy*. New York, NY: Lyle Stuart.

Emmons, R. (2010), 'Why gratitude is good', *Greater Good Magazine*, **https://greatergood.berkeley.edu/article/item/why_gratitude_is_good**

Evans, M. (2011), '23 and ½ hours', *TED-Ed Selects*, **https://ed.ted.com/featured/Mot8KdLT**

Ferguson, S. J. and Goodwin, A. D. (2010), 'Optimism and well-being in older adults: the mediating role of social support and perceived control', *International Journal of Aging and Human Development*, 71, (1), 43–68.

Foresight Mental Capital and Wellbeing Project (2008), 'Final project report – Executive summary'. London: The Government Office for Science, Crown Copyright, **www.gov.uk/government/uploads/system/uploads/attachment_data/file/292453/mental-capital-wellbeing-summary.pdf**

Fowler, J. H. and Christakis, N. A. (2010), 'Cooperative behavior cascades in human social networks', *Proceedings of the National Academy of Sciences of the United States of America*, 107, (12), 5334–8.

Frankl, V. E. (1946), *Man's Search for Meaning*. Boston, MA: Beacon Press.

Fredrickson, B. L. (2013), 'Positive emotions broaden and build', *Advances in Experimental Social Psychology*, 47, 1–53.

Fredrickson, B. L., Cohn, M. A., Coffey, K. A., Pek, J. and Finkel, S. M. (2008), 'Open hearts build lives: positive emotions, induced through loving-kindness meditation, build consequential personal resources', *Journal of Personality and Social Psychology*, 95, (5), 1045–62.

Gerhardt, S. (2014), *Why Love Matters: How Affection Shapes a Baby's Brain* (second edn). Abingdon: Routledge.

Goldman, R. and Papson, S. (1999), *Nike Culture: The Sign of the Swoosh*. London: Sage.

Goleman, D. (2015), *A Force for Good: The Dalai Lama's Vision for Our World*. London: Bloomsbury.

Gopnik, A. (2016), *The Gardener and the Carpenter: What the New Science of Child Development Tells Us About the Relationship Between Parents and Children*. London: The Bodley Head.

Gottman, J. M. (1994), *Why Marriages Succeed or Fail: And How You Can Make Yours Last*. New York, NY: Simon & Schuster.

Gowin, J. (2010), 'Why your brain needs water', *Psychology Today*, **www. psychologytoday.com/blog/you-illuminated/201010/ why-your-brain-needs-water**

Green, H., McGinnity, À., Meltzer, H., Ford, T. and Goodman, R. (2005), 'Mental health of children and young people in Great Britain, 2004'. Basingstoke: Palgrave MacMillan, Crown Copyright.

Gutman, L. M. and Vorhaus, J. (2012), 'The impact of pupil behaviour and wellbeing on educational outcomes', *DfE research report* DFE-RR253.

Hamilton, D. R. (2017), *The Five Side Effects of Kindness: This Book Will Make You Feel Better, Be Happier and Live Longer*. London: Hay House UK.

Hanson, R. (2009), *Buddha's Brain: The Practical Neuroscience of Happiness, Love and Wisdom*. Oakland, CA: New Harbinger Publications.

Hanson, R. (2014), *Hardwiring Happiness: How to Reshape Your Brain and Your Life*. London: Rider.

Health and Safety Executive (2017), 'Work-related stress, depression or anxiety statistics in Great Britain 2017', Crown Copyright, **www.hse.gov.uk/ statistics/causdis/stress/stress.pdf**

His Holiness the Dalai Lama and Cutler, H. C. (1999), *The Art of Happiness: A Handbook for Living*. London: Hodder and Stoughton.

Hulleman, C. S. and Harackiewicz, J. M. (2009), 'Promoting interest and performance in high school science classes', *Science*, 326, (5958), 1410–12.

Hume, D. (1826), *The Philosophical Works of David Hume* (Volume 3). Edinburgh: Adam Black and William Tait.

Institute of Child Education and Psychology (ICEP), *Teaching Happiness: Positive psychology for behaviour and learning, Module 2: Positive psychology in the classroom.*

Institute of Child Education and Psychology (ICEP), *Teaching Happiness: Positive psychology for behaviour and learning, Module 3: Mobilising motivation and signature strengths.*

Institute of Medicine (2013), 'Educating the student body: taking physical activity and physical education to school'. Washington, DC: National Academy of Sciences, **www.nationalacademies.org/hmd/Reports/ 2013/Educating-the-Student-Body-Taking-Physical-Activity-and- Physical-Education-to-School/Report-Brief052313.aspx**

Jenkin, M. (2014), 'How two minutes of mindfulness can calm a class and boost attainment', *The Guardian*, **www.theguardian.com/teacher-network/ teacher-blog/2014/jun/03/mindfulness-class-students-education**

Kabat-Zinn, J. (2013), *Full Catastrophe Living: How to Cope With Stress, Pain and Illness Using Mindfulness Meditation* (revised edn). London: Piatkus.

Kahneman, D. (2011), *Thinking, Fast and Slow*. London: Penguin.

Kahneman, D., Fredrickson, B. L., Schreiber, C. A. and Redelmeier, D. A. (1993), 'When more pain is preferred to less: adding a better end', *American Psychological Society*, 4, (6), 401–5.

Kaufer, D. (2011), 'What can neuroscience research teach us about teaching?'. *Presentation to the How Students Learn Working Group, 25ᵗʰ Jan 2011*, **http://gsi.berkeley.edu/programs-services/hsl-project/hsl-speakers/kaufer/**

Kell, E. (2018), *How to Survive in Teaching: Without Imploding, Exploding or Walking Away*. London: Bloomsbury Education.

Kessler, R. C., Berglund, P., Demler, O., Jin, R., Merikangas, K. R. and Walters, E. E. (2005), 'Lifetime prevalence and age-of-onset distributions of DSM-IV disorders in the National Comorbidity Survey Replication', *Archives of General Psychiatry*, 62, (6), 593–602.

Killingsworth, M. A. and Gilbert, D. T. (2010), 'A wandering mind is an unhappy mind', *Science*, 330, (6006), 932.

King, V. (2016), *10 Keys to Happier Living: A Practical Handbook for Happiness*. London: Headline Publishing Group.

Kuyken, W., Weare, K., Ukoumunne, O. C., Vicary, R., Motton, N., Burnett, R., Cullen, C., Hennelly, S. and Huppert, F. (2013), 'Effectiveness of the Mindfulness in Schools Programme: non-randomised controlled feasibility study', *The British Journal of Psychiatry*, 203, (2), 126–31.

Lally, P., van Jaarsveld, C. H. M., Potts, H. W. W. and Wardle, J. (2010), 'How are habits formed: modelling habit formation in the real world', *European Journal of Social Psychology*, 40, (6), 998–1009.

Langer, E. J. and Rodin, J. (1976), 'The effects of choice and enhanced personal responsibility for the aged: a field experiment in an institutional setting', *Journal of Personality and Social Psychology*, 34, (2), 191–8.

Layard, R., Clark, A. E., Cornaglia, F., Powdthavee, N. and Vernoit, J. (2013), 'What predicts a successful life? A life-course model of well-being', *Centre for Economic Performance*, Discussion Paper No 1245, **http://cep.lse.ac.uk/pubs/download/dp1245.pdf**

Lee, J., Tsunetsugu, Y., Takayama, N., Park, B., Li, Q., Song, C., Komatsu, M., Ikei, H., Tyrväinen, L., Kagawa, T. and Miyazaki, Y. (2014), 'Influence of forest therapy on cardiovascular relaxation in young adults', *Evidence-Based Complementary and Alternative Medicine*, 2014, 834360.

Lehrer, J. (2012), *Imagine: How Creativity Works*. New York, NY: Houghton Mifflin Harcourt.

London Playing Fields Foundation (2016), 'Coppermile: implementing a daily exercise programme at Coppermill Primary School', **https://lpff.org.uk/frontend/pdf/CoppermileEvaluationReport.pdf**

Lutz, A., Brefczynski-Lewis, J., Johnstone, T. and Davidson, R. J. (2008), 'Regulation of the neural circuitry of emotion by compassion meditation: effects of meditative expertise', *PLoS ONE*, 3, (3), e1897.

Lykken, D. and Tellegen, A. (1996), 'Happiness is a stochastic phenomenon', *Psychological Science*, 7, (3), 186–9.

Lyubomirsky, S. (2006), 'Is it possible to become lastingly happier? Answers from the modern science of well-being'. In *Vancouver Dialogues* (pp. 53–6). Vancouver: Truffle Tree Publishing.

Lyubomirsky, S. (2007), *The How of Happiness: A Practical Guide to Getting the Life You Want*. London: Piatkus.

Lyubomirsky, S., Sheldon, K. M. and Schkade, D. (2005), 'Pursuing happiness: the architecture of sustainable change', *Review of General Psychology*, 9, (2), 111–31.

Maguire, E. A., Gadian, D. G., Johnsrude, I. S., Good, C. D., Ashburner, J., Frackowiak, R. S. J. and Frith, C. D. (2000), 'Navigation-related structural change in the hippocampi of taxi drivers', *Proceedings of the National Academy of Sciences*, 97, (8), 4398–403.

Main, E. (2017), *Does Mindfulness Training Affect Levels Of Self-Regulation In Children Aged 8 – 11?* (undergraduate thesis). University of Portsmouth.

MAPPG (2015), 'Mindful Nation UK: Report by the Mindfulness All-Party Parliamentary Group (MAPPG)'. London: The Mindfulness Initiative, **www.themindfulnessinitiative.org.uk/images/reports/Mindfulness-APPG-Report_Mindful-Nation-UK_Oct2015.pdf**

Marsh, S. (2017), 'Tens of thousands of under-18s on antidepressants in England', *The Guardian*, **www.theguardian.com/society/2017/jun/18/number-of-under-18s-on-antidepressants-in-england-rises-by-12**

McGaugh, J. L. (2004), 'The amygdala modulates the consolidation of memories of emotionally arousing experiences', *Annual Review of Neuroscience*, 27, 1–28.

McGaugh, J. L., Introini-Collison, I. B., Cahill, L. F., Castellano, C., Dalmaz, C., Parent, M. B. and Williams, C. L. (1993), 'Neuromodulatory systems and memory storage: role of the amygdala', *Behavioural Brain Research*, 58, (1–2), 81–90.

McGlone, M. S. and Tofighbakhsh, J. (2000), 'Birds of a feather flock conjointly (?): rhyme as reason in aphorisms', *Psychological Science*, 11, (5), 424–8.

Montgomery, C. (2015), *Happy City: Transforming Our Lives Through Urban Design*. London: Penguin.

NASUWT (2016), 'Urgent action needed to reduce stress faced by teachers', **www.nasuwt.org.uk/article-listing/action-needed-to-reduce-stress-faced-by-teachers.html**

NHS Choices (2015), 'Benefits of exercise', **www.nhs.uk/Livewell/fitness/Pages/whybeactive.aspx**

Nitschke, J. B., Nelson, E. E., Rusch, B. D., Fox, A. S., Oakes, T. R. and Davidson, R. J. (2004), 'Orbitofrontal cortex tracks positive mood in mothers viewing pictures of their newborn infants', *Neuroimage*, 21, (2), 583–92.

Nuffield Foundation (2012), 'Social trends and mental health: Introducing the main findings'. London: Nuffield Foundation.

Nussbaum, A. D. and Dweck, C. S. (2008), 'Defensiveness versus remediation: self-theories and modes of self-esteem maintenance', *Personality and Social Psychology Bulletin*, 34, (5), 599–612.

OECD (2017), *PISA 2015 Results (Volume III): Students' Well-Being*. Paris: PISA, OECD Publishing, **www.oecd.org/pisa/PISA-2015-Results-Students-Well-being-Volume-III-Overview.pdf**

Oliner, S. (1999), 'Extraordinary acts of ordinary people: faces of heroism and altruism', *Empathy, Altruism and Agape*, **www.altruisticlove.org/docs/s_oliner.html**

Oliver, M. (1992), *House of Light*. Boston, MA: Beacon Press.

Park, N. and Peterson, C. (2006), 'Character strengths and happiness among young children: content analysis of parental descriptions', *Journal of Happiness Studies*, 7, (3), 323–41.

Park, N. and Peterson, C. (2009), 'Strengths of character in schools'. In Gilman, R., Huebner, E. S. and Furlong, M. J. (Eds.), *Handbook of Positive Psychology in Schools* (pp. 65–76). New York, NY: Routledge.

Parry-Langdon, N. (ed.) (2008), 'Three years on: survey of the development and emotional wellbeing of children and young people'. London: Office for National Statistics.

Public Health England (2014), *The Link Between Pupil Health and Wellbeing and Attainment: A Briefing for Headteachers, Governors and Staff in Education Settings*, Crown Copyright, **www.gov.uk/government/uploads/system/uploads/attachment_data/file/370686/HT_briefing_layoutvFINALvii.pdf**

Public Health England (2017), *Health Matters: Obesity and the Food Environment*, Crown Copyright, **www.gov.uk/government/publications/health-matters-obesity-and-the-food-environment/health-matters-obesity-and-the-food-environment--2**

Quoidbach, J., Wood, A. M. and Hansenne, M. (2009), 'Back to the future: the effect of daily practice of mental time travel into the future on happiness and anxiety', *The Journal of Positive Psychology*, 4, (5), 349–55.

Ratey, J. J. (2003), *A User's Guide To The Brain*. London: Abacus.

Ratey, J. J. and Hagerman, E. (2010), *Spark! How Exercise Will Improve the Performance of Your Brain*. London: Quercus.

Ratey, J. J. (2012), 'Run, jump, learn! How exercise can transform our schools', *TEDx Talk*, **tedxmanhattanbeach.com/past-events/october-2012-conference-journey-to-purpose/presenters/john-ratey**

Richerson, P. J. and Boyd, R. (1998), 'The evolution of human ultra-sociality'. In Eibl-Eibisfeldt, I. and Salter, F. (Eds.), *Indoctrinability, Ideology, and Warfare: Evolutionary Perspectives* (pp. 71–96). New York, NY: Berghahn.

Rilling, J., Gutman, D., Zeh, T., Pagnoni, G., Berns, G. and Kilts, C. (2002), 'A neural basis for social cooperation', *Neuron*, 35, (2), 395–405.

Robinson, K. (2006), 'Do schools kill creativity?', *TED Talk*, **www.ted.com/talks/ken_robinson_says_schools_kill_creativity**

Robinson, K. (2010), *The Element: How Finding Your Passion Changes Everything*. London: Penguin.

Rowling, J. K. (2008), 'The fringe benefits of failures, and the importance of imagination.' Annual Meeting of the Harvard Alumni Association.

Ryan, R. M. and Powelson, C. L. (1991), 'Autonomy and relatedness as fundamental to motivation and education', *The Journal of Experimental Education*, 60, (1), 49–66.

Schnall, S. and Roper, J. (2011), 'Elevation puts moral values into action', *Social Psychological and Personality Science*, 3, (3), 373–8.

Schwartz, B., Ward, A., Monterosso, J., Lyubomirsky, S., White, K. and Lehman, D. R. (2002), 'Maximizing versus satisficing: happiness is a matter of choice', *Journal of Personality and Social Psychology*, 83, (5), 1178–97.

Seagal, Z. V., Williams, J. M. G. and Teasdale, J. D. (2002), *Mindfulness-Based Cognitive Therapy for Depression: A New Approach to Preventing Relapse*. New York, NY: The Guildford Press.

Seligman, M. (2002), *Authentic Happiness: Using the New Positive Psychology to Realise Your Potential for Lasting Fulfilment*. New York, NY: Atria Paperback.

Seligman, M. (2011), *Flourish: A New Understanding of Happiness and Wellbeing – and How to Achieve Them*. London; Boston, MA: Nicholas Brealey Publishing.

Seligman, M. and Csikszentmihalyi, M. (2000), 'Positive psychology: an introduction', *American Psychologist*, 55, (1), 5–14.

Seligman, M., Ernst, R. M., Gillham, J., Reivich, K. and Linkins, M. (2009), 'Positive education: positive psychology and classroom interventions', *Oxford Review of Education*, 35, (3), 293–311.

Seligman, M., Steen, T. A., Park, N. and Peterson, C. (2005), 'Positive psychology progress: empirical validation of interventions', *American Psychologist*, 60, (5), 410–21.

Service, O., Hallsworth, M., Halpern, D., Algate, F., Gallagher, R., Nguyen, S., Ruda, S. and Sanders, M. (2015), 'EAST: four simple ways to apply behavioural insights'. London: The Behavioural Insights Team.

Sheldon, K. M. and Lyubomirsky, S. (2007), 'Is it possible to become happier? (And if so, how?)', *Social and Personality Psychology Compass*, 1, (1), 129–45.

Slatcher, R. B. and Pennebaker, J. W. (2006), 'How do I love thee? Let me count the words: the social effects of expressive writing', *Psychological Science*, 17, (8), 660–4.

Smith, J. L., Harrison, P. R., Kurtz, J. L. and Bryant, F. B. (2014), 'Nurturing the capacity to savor: interventions to enhance the enjoyment of positive experiences'. In Parks, A. C. and Schueller, S. M. (Eds.), *The Wiley Blackwell Handbook of Positive Psychological Interventions*. Hoboken: Wiley-Blackwell.

Snel, E. (2013), *Sitting Still Like a Frog: Mindfulness Exercises for Kids (and Their Parents)*. Boulder, CO: Shambhala Publications.

Speer, M. E. and Delgado, M. R. (2017), 'Reminiscing about positive memories buffers acute stress responses', *Nature Human Behaviour*, 1, 0093.

Suttie, J. (2012), 'Can schools helps students find flow?', *Greater Good Magazine*, **www.greatergood.berkeley.edu/article/item/can_schools_help_students_find_flow**

Szeto, A., Nation, D. A., Mendez, A. J., Dominguez-Bendala, J., Brooks, L. G., Schneiderman, N. and McCabe, P. M. (2008), 'Oxytocin attenuates NADPH-dependent superoxide activity and IL-6 secretion in macrophages and vascular cells', *American Journal of Physiology. Endocrinology and Metabolism*, 295, (6), E1495–501.

Tamir, M., Schwartz, S., Oishi, S. and Kim, M. Y. (2017), 'The secret to happiness: feeling good or feeling right?', *Journal of Experimental Psychology*, 146, (10), 1448–59.

The Children's Society (2016), 'The Good Childhood Report 2016: Summary', **www.childrenssociety.org.uk/sites/default/files/pcr090_summary_web.pdf**

The Daily Mile (2018), 'Health and wellbeing', **https://thedailymile.co.uk/health-wellbeing**

Townsend, N., Wickramasinghe, K., Williams, J., Bhatnagar, P. and Rayner, M. (2015), *Physical Activity Statistics 2015*. London: British Heart Foundation.

UK Government (2011), *Physical Activity Guidelines for Children and Young People (5–18 Years)*, Crown Copyright, **www.gov.uk/government/uploads/system/uploads/attachment_data/file/213739/dh_128144.pdf**

UK Government (2017), *Childhood Obesity: A Plan for Action*, Crown copyright, **www.gov.uk/government/publications/childhood-obesity-a-plan-for-action/childhood-obesity-a-plan-for-action**

Ulrich, R. S. (1984), 'View through a window may influence recovery from surgery', *Science*, 224, 420–1.

Vickery, C. E. and Dorjee, D. (2016), 'Mindfulness training in primary schools decreases negative affect and increases meta-cognition in children', *Frontiers in Psychology*, 6, 2025.

Waters, E., Wippman, J. and Sroufe, L. A. (1979), 'Attachment, positive affect, and competence in the peer group: two studies in construct validation', *Child Development*, 50, (3), 821–9.

Way, B. M., Creswell, J. D., Eisenberger, N. I. and Lieberman, M. D. (2010), 'Dispositional mindfulness and depressive symptomatology: correlations with limbic and self-referential neural activity during rest', *Emotion*, 10, (1), 12–24.

Weale, S. (2016), 'Almost a third of teachers quit state sector within five years of qualifying', *The Guardian*, **www.theguardian.com/education/ 2016/oct/24/almost-third-of-teachers-quit-within-five-years-of- qualifying-figures**

Weng, H.Y., Fox, A. S., Shackman, A. J., Stodola, D. E., Caldwell, J. Z. K., Olson, M. C., Rogers, G. M. and Davidson, R. J. (2013), 'Compassion training alters altruism and neural responses to suffering', *Psychological Science*, 24, (7), 1171–80.

What Works Centre for Wellbeing (2017), 'Sport, dance and young people', **https://whatworkswellbeing.files.wordpress.com/2017/06/dance- sport-wellbeing-briefing-22june.pdf**

Williams, M. and Penman, D. (2011), *Mindfulness: A Practical Guide to Finding Peace in a Frantic World*. London: Piatkus.

Winnicott, D. W. (1962), *The Child and the Family: First Relationships*. London: Tavistock.

Yerkes, R. M. and Dodson, J. D. (1908), 'The relation of strength of stimulus to rapidity of habit-formation', *Journal of Comparative Neurology and Psychology*, 18, (5), 459–82.

Youth Sport Trust (2015), 'YST national PE, school sport and physical activity survey report', **www.youthsporttrust.org/sites/yst/files/resources/ pdf/national_pe__school_sport_and_physical_activity_survey_ report.pdf**

Index

Note: Page numbers in *italics* denote figures.